Stephanie Alexander

A Shared Table

Stephanie

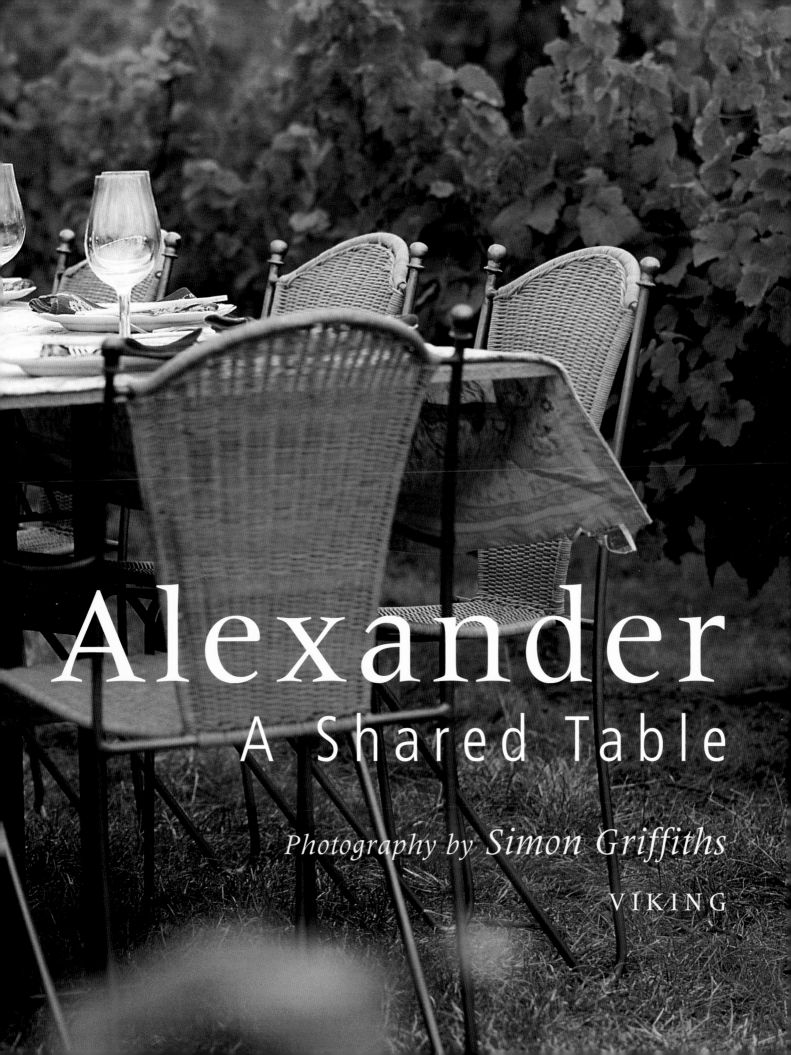

Alexander
A Shared Table

Photography by Simon Griffiths

VIKING

ACKNOWLEDGEMENTS

A Shared Table was always going to be a complicated combined project, resulting in this beautiful book and a seven-part television series. Simon Griffiths, the stills photographer, travelled with the crew to each location and dodged camera jibs and lights to get his wonderful shots. My marvellous assistant, Elena Bonnici, worked hard to ensure that Simon and the television crew got to see all stages of the food preparation – a very difficult task at times. The food producers we visited were patient and understanding and without exception charming, inspiring and sometimes eccentric individuals. All of the crew at December Films were fantastic as were the editorial, design and production teams at Penguin Books. Once again Julie Gibbs has overseen another ambitious and beautiful book. What a journey it was and how lovely it is to have such a stunning record of our culinary odyssey. Thank you to everyone involved.

Cheese tasting notes from *Chalk and Cheese* by Will Studd reprinted with permission from Purple Egg.
'Passionfruit' by Chris Wallace-Crabbe from *Rungs of Time* reprinted with permission from Oxford University Press.
Sponge cake on page 105 made by Country Style Homemade Cakes, Freshwater Creek, Victoria.

Front cover: Artichokes from George Biron's garden at Sunnybrae, near Birregurra, Victoria.
Front flap: Braised artichokes (see page 79).
Back flap: Gathering tetragonia on Kangaroo Island.
Back cover: Rock lobster from Kangaroo Island.
Endpapers: Sunset at Snelling Beach, Kangaroo Island.
Half-title page: Stephanie Alexander and Elena Bonnici in Stephanie's kitchen, Melbourne.
Title page: Table set for lunch at Pipers Brook Vineyard, Tasmania.
Dedication page: After making filo pastry in Janni Kyritsis's kitchen, Sydney.

Viking
Penguin Books Australia Ltd
487 Maroondah Highway, PO Box 257
Ringwood, Victoria 3134, Australia
Penguin Books Ltd
Harmondsworth, Middlesex, England
Penguin Putnam Inc.
375 Hudson Street, New York, New York 10014, USA
Penguin Books Canada Limited
10 Alcorn Avenue, Toronto, Ontario, Canada M4V 3B2
Penguin Books (N.Z.) Ltd
Cnr Rosedale and Airborne Roads, Albany, Auckland
New Zealand
Penguin Books (South Africa) (Pty) Ltd
5 Watkins Street, Denver Ext 4, 2094, South Africa
Penguin Books India (P) Ltd
11, Community Centre, Panchsheel Park
New Delhi 110 017, India

First published by Penguin Books Australia Ltd 1999

10 9 8 7 6 5 4 3 2 1

Designed by Ruth Grüner, Tony Palmer
and Judith Grace
Photography by Simon Griffiths, except photographs on pages 110–11 (Stock Photos), 178–9 (Andrew Chapman), 181 (The Photo Library) and 220 (Stock Photos)
Maps drawn by Michelle Katsouranis

Typeset in Meridien and Frutiger by Ruth Grüner, Stephen Chan and Sandra Sheehan
Printed in Australia by Sands Print Group, Geelong, Victoria

National Library of Australia
Cataloguing-in-Publication data:

Alexander, Stephanie, 1940– .
    A shared table.

    Includes index.
    ISBN 0 670 88663 7.

    1. Gastronomy. 2. Cookery, Australian. 3. Food industry and trade – Australia. I. Griffiths, Simon (Simon John). II. Title. III. Title: A shared table (Television program).

641.50994

contents

introduction

I am still frequently asked what constitutes Australian cuisine. My answer is: diversity and energy. Travelling around the country over the past year making a television series and writing this book, I explored the Australian culinary landscape and the same things struck me over and over again. First, the variety and quality of what is available to us all, and second, the manner in which our passionate producers face up to quite awesome challenges with universal good humour in order to achieve the best possible product. The varied and stunning Australian landscapes were a constant and magnificent reminder of the link between the land, the climate and what it can produce.

In each region I devised a delicious well-balanced meal, using locally grown or reared foods. I visited the farms and the orchards, and went out on the boats. I listened carefully as the farmers, fishermen, orchardists and butchers spoke to me about how they ensure best quality. Always I learnt new things and was privileged to taste cheese just a few minutes old, or fruit picked straight from the tree, or sausages that were just ready to cut, or bread hot from the oven, or wine that was not yet released. My assistant, Elena Bonnici, and I then cooked the dishes, always with more than a little help from our friends, before sitting down to enjoy sharing the table with those who produced the food.

Elena spent two years of her cooking apprenticeship in the kitchens at Stephanie's Restaurant and moved in and out for several more years after qualifying. Within days of our first meeting I had no doubts that here was a true food lover and a natural cook. I was not so sure how long Elena would continue in this very tough profession as she learns very quickly, becomes bored easily and has a restless eye. She slips effortlessly from position to position, always charming those she works with, always giving 100 per cent, but somehow she radiates a sense of 'don't fence me in'. This project, with its inbuilt variety, excitement and demand for high quality, seemed perfect for her and she was a delightful accomplice and, as ever, a great deal of fun.

I believe that sharing good food and wine, conversation and laughter around a table is one of life's most satisfying and joyful pleasures. Many of the young people I have worked with or have come to know have surprised me with their lack of knowledge of how to prepare meals from fresh ingredients. My hope is that some of them will be inspired by the stories and photographs in this book to move into the kitchen from time to time so that they can experience the heady pleasure of sharing a table with friends, confident in having chosen and prepared fine Australian ingredients with ease and simple good taste.

PREVIOUS PAGES   The wild coastline along the Great Ocean Road in Victoria is one of the most beautiful in Australia. We travelled along it during the filming of 'A Country Cook'.

OPPOSITE AND BELOW   Scenes from the making of the television series, from left: the TV monitor at Queen Victoria Market, Melbourne; filming the lunch at Pipers Brook Vineyard, Tasmania; make-up artist Fiona Munday attends to me at Queen Victoria Market; Elena, sound recordist Paul Finlay and I in hygienic whites at the Bonlac factory, Victoria, to film the making of buffalo mozzarella.

out west

Western Australia's South-West

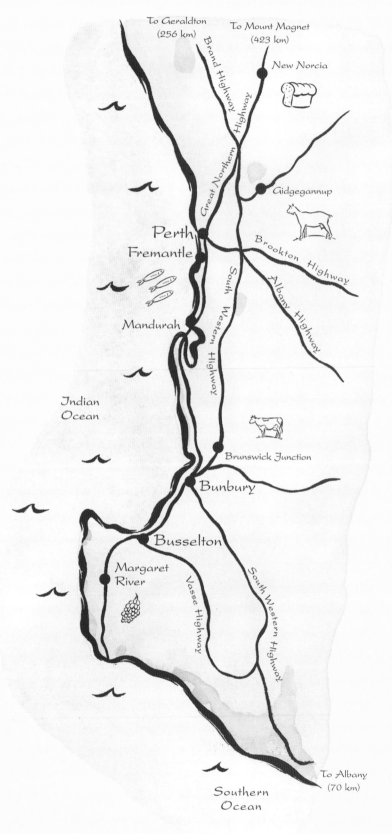

To Geraldton
(256 km)

To Mount Magnet
(423 km)

Brand Highway

Great Northern Highway

New Norcia

Gidgegannup

Perth

Fremantle

Brookton Highway

South Western Highway

Albany Highway

Mandurah

Indian Ocean

Brunswick Junction

Bunbury

Busselton

Margaret River

Vasse Highway

South Western Highway

To Albany
(70 km)

Southern Ocean

Yesterday in the late afternoon I watched the seafoam curl creamily onto the white sand at Cottesloe Beach as I waited for the sun to set over the sea – a special sight for someone from the east. Whenever the sun shines in Perth, and it does on a good many days of the year, it seems like a great idea to gather a few friends and indulge in a long, lazy lunch. Today is just such a day. A generous friend has offered his garden and impressive kitchen. We shall set the table with handpainted plates from La Maiolica in Fremantle. Elena and I will cook with a little help from our friends. Every dish and every guest has a story worth telling.

Vince | *Vince Garreffa has been a friend and a much-valued supplier since we met more than eight years ago when I first explored the food resources of this exciting state.* He and his wife, Ann, are generous with hospitality whenever a visiting food lover comes their way. Vince is an entrepreneurial butcher but, more than that, he is a man who recognises and appreciates top quality. He is passionate about good food. Together with his friend John Maiorana, a former mathematics teacher, the two are never happier than when they are cooking together. Such events are always at Vince's home in the Perth suburb of Mount Lawley in order to take full advantage of the custom-built 3-metre-long range Vince has in his kitchen – big enough to roast an entire lamb. On this visit Vince and Ann offered us their home in which to cook our special Western Australian lunch. It was a memorable occasion.

For many years Vince has supplied me with exceptional veal, known as White Rocks veal. This time I wanted to understand its story better and Vince agreed to take me to see for myself. White Rocks veal is a rosy pink. European veal is pale pink; in times gone by it was a product of animals wintering indoors close to their mothers and as such was entirely milk-fed and a strictly seasonal product. To cope with demand European veal producers devised methods of producing this meat all year round, often in rather horrible conditions from the calf's point of view. All of this was in my mind as I rather nervously set out for the dairy farm at Brunswick Junction, owned for three generations by the Partridge family.

PREVIOUS PAGES   White Rocks veal is raised in the lush green countryside south of Perth.
BELOW   The sun sets over Fremantle's tranquil harbour.

WHITE ROCKS DAIRY FARM

David and Lizzie | *David and Lizzie Partridge's dairy farm at Brunswick Junction is within the Shire of Harvey, 160 kilometres south of Perth, known throughout the state as prime cattle and dairy country.* Their son Michael is now taking over the day-to-day management of the farm. Easterners sometimes have a stereotypical image of all the west as bone-dry and brown. The further one moves towards the south-west corner the less apt is this picture. The paddocks we passed were green and lush. It was raining gently and the mud was richly red and very sticky. 'Mud is money. If there's no mud there's dust and no money,' said David happily.

White Rocks Dairy Farm was founded in 1887 by John Partridge, the grandfather and great-grandfather of the present owners. David described how his grandfather had constructed the original house in 1889 using pitsawn timber. A tree was felled and lay too heavy to be moved, so a hole or pit was dug underneath, the length of the log. One man jumped into the pit and another stayed on top and together they worked the long saw to slice through the length of the log, and so on and so on to make suitable planks for the walls of the cottage.

White Rocks has always been a dairy farm and began sending milk to Perth (in milk cans wrapped in wet bags) as soon as the railway line opened in 1894. These days the dairy is absolutely state-of-the-art, with a rotating milking stand for fifty cows where each animal is fitted with a transponder to allow electronic identification and computerised feeding to her individual requirement. The milk is pumped into instantly chilled milk tanks – a far cry from the days of milk cans and wet bags.

The system for selling milk is different in the west than in the eastern states. Once the milk contract is filled and this milk is sold for the highest price, it is up to

the farmer to dispose of the rest of his production at lesser prices, even though the quality remains constant. At White Rocks Dairy Farm some of the milk is sold on to make simple cheeses, such as mascarpone, and flavoured milk, but a radical departure was the Partridges' decision to invest in the rearing of milk-fed calves. One thousand litres a day of best-quality milk is currently consumed by the growing calves. Before this decision was made calves were slaughtered at one to two weeks of age, producing veal of very poor quality (still sold in the markets as 'bobby veal'). The calves are now kept for three to four months and produce superb veal.

As with so many intelligent farmers today, David considers ecological issues of paramount importance. He explained his system of controlling effluent from the farm. All manure is spread around the paddocks and the diluted effluent is used to irrigate the farm. 'Farmers should go to jail if their effluent gets into the water-ways,' says David.

Both David and Lizzie are keenly aware of their heritage. Amid all this very state-of-the-art plant Lizzie has established a small museum of artefacts, which allows visitors (tourists and schoolchildren and pensioners) either to indulge in a little nostalgia or to understand better how things used to be done. The museum is housed partly in an old worker's cottage built in 1891, still in its original position on the farm, while the very special dairy collection is displayed in an old schoolhouse that David and Lizzie saved from demolition and had transported to their farm. A few agricultural machines of an early vintage are displayed on the grassy bank outside the cottage. David says sometimes visiting pensioners sit in the iron saddle of a plough for an hour or two smiling and remembering their more energetic years.

I love looking at well-worn reminders of past lives. Here were kitchen sieves and iron pots and a genuine Coolgardie meat safe and a chip bath heater and much more. I was intrigued to read an entry in a cash book from an early household showing that in 1896 weekly purchases came to £2.13.3 and items purchased included sheeting, syrup, soda, calico, candles, tobacco and rice. The dairy collection included smooth butter pats, butter churns, butter stamps, butter scoops and curd skimmers. There was a superbly crafted butter worker, and a smooth and shallow bowl fitted with a paddle turned from softly golden Huon pine. Some very early iron curd cutters and wooden cheese presses told of early cheesemaking.

It was time to visit the calves. A rich smell of manure surrounded the sheds. Several calves share the same pen and remain together for all of their lives. They have room to move about and lie down. The stall walls are about a metre high. Fresh air circulates and there is plenty of natural light.

European horror stories tell of calves fed on powdered milk or milk substitute and on hormones without enough iron to enable them to stand, housed in pens too small for them to lie down and deprived of fresh air and light. The situation was quite different at White Rocks. David told me proudly: 'These calves are fed no

OPPOSITE   White Rocks Dairy Farm is named for the towering craggy boulders that mark the entrance to the 525-hectare property.

ABOVE   Currently around 400 cows are milked at White Rocks, of which the majority are top-quality Friesians.

OVERLEAF   Lizzie Partridge's museum of kitchen artefacts allows visitors to look back at the heritage of Australia's white settlers.

hormones or antibiotics, but they do have warm milk from top-quality Friesian cows on tap with rubber nipples let into the pens so the animals can feed at will. From three weeks of age they also have some lightly rolled barley and lupin to give them adequate iron. They grow at an average of 1 kilogram a day.'

David rubbed the nose of the nearest calf. No amount of wishful thinking can disguise the fact that these animals only look forward to a short life (about twelve weeks) and will never experience the delights of living among green grass. But farmers are realists and no good farmer would tolerate cruelty to his animals. From a practical point of view stressed animals produce tough meat and the quality of this veal is superb – and that is from one who has consumed a good deal of it.

There are those who take exception to the issue of raising any animals to provide meat for humans, and to the existence of broadacre farming to support such animal rearing. I am not one of them. Instead I am interested and intrigued to listen to farmers discuss questions of value-adding in today's farm environment, the role of technology and the implications of change, the fact that viability depends on quality and successful marketing, the necessity for diversification, and the ever-increasing importance of Quality Assurance programs at all points in the food chain.

OPPOSITE AND ABOVE The main dish at our lunch was the classic and splendid roast veal, accompanied by slow-braised vegetables (see page 14) and dried figs.

Roasted rack of veal

1 rack veal
6 cloves garlic, unpeeled
4 small sprigs rosemary *or* a few fennel leaves
sea salt
freshly ground black pepper
olive oil
4 large sweet onions, unpeeled and halved
   crosswise *or* 8 small onions, peeled
4 medium-sized potatoes, unpeeled and halved
2 cups light chicken *or* veal stock mixed with
   1 glass dry white wine

❧ SERVES 8

Preheat oven to 180°C. Peel and finely slice two of the garlic cloves. Make a tiny nick between each veal rib bone and tuck in a sliver of the sliced garlic and a bit of rosemary or fennel. Season the rack well and rub all over with oil. Rub a baking dish with more oil and settle the meat in the dish. In the remaining spaces

arrange the oiled onion and potato halves. The unpeeled garlic and any remaining rosemary or fennel should be thrown in too.

Bake for 1 hour, basting every 15 minutes with 2 tablespoons of the stock and wine mix. After an hour test the meat by plunging a very fine skewer into its thickest part and leaving it there for 30 seconds. Note if the juice that oozes from the cut is a very pale pink or clear and then touch the skewer to your lip. If it is quite warm, the roast is ready.

Remove the rack and vegetables to a hot dish and loosely cover with aluminium foil to keep warm while you deglaze the pan with the remainder of the stock and wine mixture. This simple roasting juice is quite delicious and to my mind needs no thickening. Add to it any juices that ooze from the resting meat and pour over to serve.

Vince demonstrated how to trim a rack properly so that one can cut effortlessly between the bones. All of these trimmings are very valuable for stock, either to make immediately if the preparation is several hours before the meal, or to bag, label and freeze. Any rib-bone section that is sawn away by the butcher can be used similarly.

Slow-braised vegetables

I find it hard to resist big flat meaty mushrooms, and for our lunch they were delicious in among the veal juices. There is no need to peel them as far as edibility goes but if you want them to absorb the flavour of extra-virgin olive oil, do peel them and then brush them generously with the oil, grind some pepper over and place under a preheated grill or on a barbecue. Once juicy and smelling wonderful, squeeze over a few drops of lemon juice and sprinkle with a very little sea salt.

Options for this recipe might be whole witlof or whole, halved or quartered fennel bulbs, trimmed hearts of artichoke, young turnips, sweet small onions, and so on. The dish can accompany roast meat, as in our lunch, but on another occasion you might serve the braise in slightly larger quantities without need of any other dish – most appropriate if you have offered a substantial first course.

1 whole witlof *or* 1 whole or 2 half fennel bulbs *or* 1–2 artichokes per person, depending on size of vegetables
stock and white wine (mixed as for the roast veal on page 13)
salt and pepper
fresh herbs of your choice (to complement the flavours in the veal)

Preheat the oven to 180°C. Butter or oil an ovenproof dish that will hold all the vegetables firmly in one layer. Position the witlof, fennel or artichokes in the dish and moisten with liquid to come halfway up the vegetables. Cover with buttered or oiled aluminium foil, pressing it down, to slow down the evaporation of the cooking juices.

If serving with the veal on page 13, most of the suggested vegetables should be put into the oven at the same time as the meat. Bake for 45 minutes and check for doneness – the vegetables may well need a full hour.

Successful braising depends on there being just the right amount of liquid so that the vegetables are kept moist, but do not swim. When the vegetables are completely tender they should be sitting in their own concentrated juices. Braised vegetables are *never* crunchy!

Piccata of veal with lemon juice and crisped sage

4 tablespoons unsalted butter

1 bunch sage, leaves picked from the stems *or*

    40 garden-picked sage leaves

8 x 60 g thin slices veal

2 tablespoons plain flour, seasoned with a little

    salt and pepper

2 tablespoons extra-virgin olive oil

juice of 1 lemon

2 tablespoons chopped parsley

SERVES 4

Melt half the butter in a non-stick frying pan and drop in the sage leaves. Over a moderate heat and using a slotted spoon, keep the leaves turning until they are crisp. Lift them out quickly, drain on kitchen paper and keep in a warm place. Wipe out the frying pan.

Dip the veal slices into the seasoned flour and shake off the excess. Heat half the oil with the remaining butter until the foam is just starting to disperse and then fry half the veal, turning after 2 minutes on the first side. Cook a further 2 minutes, adjusting the heat if necessary so the meat does not burn. Lift out the veal and keep warm on a heated plate. Wipe out the pan and repeat the process with the rest of the meat.

Return all the veal to the pan. Increase the heat a little. Squeeze over the lemon juice and scatter with parsley. Turn each veal piece so it gets its share of parsley and lemon. Transfer at once to a serving platter on which braised vegetables (or boiled potatoes for a simpler presentation) are waiting, and scatter the lot with the sage leaves.

To serve. Cook a combination of slow-braised vegetables as described on page 14. Pile these sticky, delicious shapes with all their juices into the centre of a heated platter, tuck the quick-sautéed small pieces of veal around the vegetables and scatter all with the crisped sage leaves.

It is a nice surprise to reverse the balance so often chosen in Australian homes and make vegetables the star of this dish, but its success lies with the quality of the meat. It must be tender and it must be cut from a single muscle. If the meat has not been cut from a single muscle it will curl and distort in the pan. Vince recommends the girello of White Rocks veal or the round from the leg. In the latter case he would cut the slices into small medallions.

White Rocks butter

I copied down these instructions for making butter from a photocopy of an old recipe displayed on the dairy wall at White Rocks. It said you would need a beater, ice, salt, butter pats, knives, a tray, a jug (for buttermilk), tea towels, a handtowel and an apron.

1 bowl hot water

1 bowl cold iced water

1 bowl cream

1/4 teaspoon salt

Beat the cream to an almost butter-like consistency. Dip your hands into the hot water and then the cold icy water. Squeeze the beaten cream by hand until all the buttermilk is out and you are left with the butterfat. Add the salt (more or less, to taste) to the butter. Put the butter into the cold icy water to cool (if it is too salty, wash the butter in the water longer).

Dip the butter pats into the hot water and then the cold water. Put butter onto the pats and pat into shape. This also removes any buttermilk that may still be left in the butter.

If you mix the remaining buttermilk with self-raising flour, the dough makes lovely scones to go with your freshly made butter.

OPPOSITE   We grilled fresh mushrooms (left) and braised some beautiful green fennel (right) to accompany the superb roast veal.

ABOVE   Western Australia is often hot and dry, but it is not always so. When I visited Gabrielle Kervella in winter, she was bundled up against the cold. A pale sun struggled through the clouds and the first newborn kids were a delight to see, hopping and jumping and then snuggling up to their mothers.

OPPOSITE   Gabrielle contributed exquisite individual cabecou (matured discs of goat's cheese) to our lunch.

KERVELLA CHEESE

Gabrielle | *My friend Gabrielle Kervella has her property at Gidgegannup, 60 kilometres north-east of Perth.* In 1984 Gabrielle produced the first outstanding farmhouse goat cheeses in Australia. Since then she has gone from strength to strength, winning respect from all who taste her lovely cheeses, as well as many industry awards. In 1999 Kervella Cheese was awarded the *Gourmet Traveller* Jaguar Award for Excellence in Primary Production. Her cheeses include a fromage blanc (fresh-ripened goat curd); fromage frais; an ashed cheese (cendre); her matured style, sold as affiné, which means 'matured'; and rounds of fromage frais rolled in paprika, peppercorns or herbs.

Gabrielle spent many years in France, where she developed a great passion for fine cheese. Once she moved to her property in the west she realised that it needed to be productive. She already had a few goats for milk and her thoughts turned to cheesemaking. She trained in France, with cheesemakers renowned for their goat's milk cheeses, and returned to her property to set up her own business. She quickly found that she had to breed her own goat herd to adapt to the harsher Australian conditions. Over the years she has become more and more passionate about introducing biodynamic practices as a means of achieving a balance with nature on her farm. Her milking goats are a cross between Saanen, Nubian and Alpine breeds.

My first visit had been in winter, when lush grass covered the home paddocks – a complete contrast to my more recent visit in mid-autumn when the paddocks were bleached from the summer sun. Gabrielle was now assisted by a South African cheesemaker, Alan Cockman, and his wife, Charmaine. Their two small daughters instructed Elena on how to gently herd the goats in for milking and how to milk them. Once again we discussed the philosophical beliefs that under-lie all decisions made on the farm. The lactation cycles of the goats are respected utterly, resulting in uneven production in the colder months of the year, unlike practices on some other farms where the animals' cycle is adjusted through the use of hormones to achieve year-round production. Gabrielle believes passionately that it is only by adhering to traditional methods that one can hope to achieve sustainable farm practices.

I was interested to learn that Gabrielle offers board to young people from all over the world who are members of WWOOF, an acronym that stands for 'Willing Workers on Organic Farms'. These young travellers work hard and in return see interesting parts of the country and meet Australians who are passionate about organic farming methods. Currently her WWOOFers are a Dutch lawyer and two Japanese travellers. Especially for the Japanese couple, the contrast could not be more marked between their urban, tightly controlled life at home and this completely isolated, tranquil and open environment.

Baked goat's cheese crottin

8 x 1 cm slices firm goat's cheese

clarified butter

POTATO GALETTES

1 egg yolk

1 whole egg

200 g cooked potato

200 g grated raw potato

175 g pouring cream

salt and pepper

plain flour

DRESSING

1 teaspoon chopped anchovy fillets

½ teaspoon finely chopped garlic

1 tablespoon unsalted butter

good squeeze of lemon juice

1 teaspoon roughly chopped flat-leaf parsley

〰 SERVES 4 (8 GALETTES)

To make the galettes. Place all the ingredients except the flour in a bowl. Mix together, adding just enough flour to make a mix that will hold its shape. Drop spoonfuls into a pan of hot clarified butter and fry until golden. Transfer the galettes to a paper-towel-lined tray and keep warm in the oven until ready to serve.

To make the dressing. Heat the anchovy and garlic in a small pan for 1 minute, add the butter and allow to foam. Just as it turns a light nut-brown, add the lemon juice and the parsley.

To serve. Place a slice of cheese on top of each galette and place under an overhead grill until the cheese starts to bubble and becomes golden. Transfer two galettes onto each of four hot plates and spoon over the dressing. Serve at once.

At Richmond Hill Cafe & Larder we sit our grilled goat's cheese on firm potato pancakes and serve them with some salad leaves and a little anchovy and parsley dressing.

FREMANTLE

Fremantle has almost forgotten its burst of fame during the 1983 America's Cup Challenge. Now it is concerned with promoting its special character for the long term. The sandstone buildings have all been carefully cleaned and restored, paving stones are imprinted with crabs and prawns and starfish to reinforce the nautical flavour, expensive yachts bob at anchor in the marina, and the appealing Maritime Museum attracts many tourists. It is here in Fremantle that the replica of Captain Cook's *Endeavour*, HM Bark *Endeavour*, was built. This ship sailed into Portsmouth and on up the Thames to London and a royal welcome in March 1997, 200 years after Cook first sailed into Botany Bay on the original *Endeavour*.

I wandered along the boardwalk and admired the newly constructed Harbour Apartments, built right out into the water, my home for the next few days. Olive trees flourished in the inner courtyards and canvas sails offered privacy between the decks, on which a few residents reclined on wooden steamer chairs. I stood alone, a breeze ruffling my hair, and listened to a silence broken only by the creak of boats at anchor and the soft splash of water against a jetty. And just then I heard a plaintive harmonica, being played by an unseen musician who must have been relaxing in the cabin of one of the boats at anchor. On the horizon were massed grey clouds, split by bands of bright gold as the sun slipped away.

Gigi and Cate | *Craftsman Gigi Cosi and his wife, Cate, have their workshop and retail business, La Maiolica, nearby, where they make, decorate and fire traditional majolica tableware.* I own some of these plates and every time I set a summer luncheon table in my garden I choose them and am reminded of Fremantle, and of outdoor eating on sunbleached days when the bright colours uplift the spirit and cry out for colourful salads and other simple summer dishes. Cate admits that a few new designs have been allowed to creep into the repertoire of mainly traditional Italian designs. This tableware uses the 'inglaze' technique where the colours penetrate right through the glaze. The shop attracts many visitors who wish to take home a useful and beautiful souvenir of Fremantle.

For our special lunch Gigi and Cate made a complete set of plates and bowls and jugs in summery greens and yellows and we decorated the table with bunches of lemons and lemon leaves picked from Vince's tree.

ABOVE   A craypot on the Fremantle wharf is a reminder that this port is the centre of the Western Australian fishing industry. OPPOSITE   Eighty per cent of the designs used at La Maiolica are traditional Italian designs, the geometric shapes and colours hinting at historical links with Islam and ancient Egypt.

Jim and Rosa | *Jim Mendolia embodies the spirit of Fremantle in many ways.*

Italians are important in this town. The local bocce club has pride of place on the waterfront, and many of the best locations here are owned and operated by Italian-Australian families – not forgetting the prominent Greek-Australian Kailis family. Together, the Italians and Greeks control the all-important fishing industry, fishing for line fish, rock crayfish, scallops and, in Jim's case, sardines.

Jim's brother Aldo is a rock lobster fisherman and he told me of the annual festival where the Italian cray fishermen get together at the end of the season to make new craypots from imported rattan and local soaked tea-tree stakes. Apparently it is a fun day with a large barbecue lunch served once the work is over. I mentally noted another reason to return to the west to experience this.

On the wharf Jim proudly showed me his boat, MSS *Del Tindari*, and introduced me to his *compare*, Frank Mazzeo, who had just tied up his trawler, *Sea Tang*, after a night at sea. (Jim tried to explain the complex relationship. *Compare* seems to mean something like our term 'godfather'.) Frank showed me his catch. I was especially excited by the saucer scallops, which I decided to cook for my guests for lunch the next day. Frank also had small red mullet, sole, flounder, sand whiting and sky-blue-tailed prawns. Elena and I exclaimed with pleasure at the sight of such fresh fish, still stiff with rigor mortis (the best sign of fish just caught) and with shining colours, pink, silver, and blue. We tried to buy and Frank insisted on giving us a huge bag of these treasures from the deep. 'In Italy only the doctor can eat fish like this,' said Frank. 'In Italy this mullet would cost $35 per kilo. I will be lucky to get $4 for it.'

That night back at our apartment I scaled and cleaned – rather inexpertly without proper tools – until I resembled a pearly queen or a mermaid with silvery scales stuck all over my T-shirt, and we grilled and panfried the lot. It was so balmy that we set tables on the deck and relaxed, listening to the slap of rigging and now and then a faint splash in the sea (bird? fish?), and were caressed by salty breezes. The entire television crew feasted on the morning's catch, seasoned with nothing more than olive oil, lemon juice and salt and pepper. The only extra was a bowl of boiled potatoes and a big tomato salad.

Jim Mendolia has single-handedly created a quality sardine industry in this part of the world and is the driving force behind the annual Sardine Festival. His sardine factory is worth a visit to watch the silvery fish being scaled, gutted, filleted and packed on a magic conveyer belt. Sardines are also caught, salted, filleted by hand and later packed with olive oil and marketed as Auschovies. This infant industry is creating a delicacy, using a product that for many fishermen was formerly considered only as bait. Jim offers an inspirational model for other small operators who wonder if they can diversify or succeed with an entrepreneurial venture. Jim is now experimenting with more exotic sardine preparations.

ABOVE Jim Mendolia on board the MSS *Del Tindari* (top) and his *compare*, Frank Mazzeo. OPPOSITE, CLOCKWISE FROM BELOW LEFT A fisherman weighs his catch at the wharf; freshly caught sardines; tools of Jim's trade, a filleting knife and fish hooks.

I was pleased to meet Jim's mother, Rosa, who showed me her method of pickling the delicious little sardines with chillies and fresh herbs. She had a quick and efficient method of cutting the head from each fish. Using scissors, she cut diagonally across the stomach of the fish and pulled the guts and head away from the flesh in one operation. A lift of the backbone and the fish was quite clean. She offered me some of her home-cured black olives. They were superb and I begged the recipe.

Rosa cooks lunch for Jim and his brother, Aldo, every day and after my pickled sardine lesson we all tucked into the family favourite, spaghetti and meat sauce, Sicilian-style. Chunks of meat are cooked in the tomato sauce and are then lifted out and served separately. This way of serving harks back to a time when meat was too expensive to eat in large quantities and the men, who were the breadwinners, were offered the meat first. Over lunch Jim reminisced about his childhood in Fremantle. 'We always worked,' he said. 'We went fishing after school and sold the fish and started to earn real money. It was very different to the Aussie kids.' Aldo's huge labrador, Bella, goes out on the boat every day. She has her own fishing licence and enjoys a pasta or crayfish lunch every day!

Pickled sardines with chilli

fresh sardines
salt
red-wine vinegar
a jug of olive oil
dried oregano (leaf variety, not ground powder)
roughly chopped flat-leaf parsley
sliced garlic
sliced fresh chilli

This is Rosa's recipe: 'You must start with absolutely fresh fish. Wash them, then leave them in the refrigerator for 24 hours – they will be easier to handle. Using scissors, cut off the head diagonally just under the gills and pull out the backbone. The guts will come away with the head. Sprinkle the sardines generously with kitchen salt and leave for 2 hours. Rinse off the salt and generously cover them with good wine vinegar for another 2 hours, which cooks the flesh and adds flavour. Then they must be very well drained and patted dry. [Rosa gave them a good squeeze with her hands.]

'Put some oil in a bowl followed by a layer of the drained fillets. Sprinkle over dried oregano, parsley, garlic and chilli (not too much as it can get stronger over time). Add more olive oil. Continue to layer the fillets and the flavourings until you run out of fillets. Then cover them completely with good olive oil. Keep in the refrigerator. They can be eaten within a day but they are much better after a week or two, and will last in the fridge for a year.'

Rosa's pickled olives

ripe black olives

salt

fennel seeds

sliced garlic

sliced fresh chilli

dried oregano

Place the olives on a flat, perforated tray and sit in a semi-sunny spot to dry for 10 days. Place a plate or something underneath to catch any drips, which will stain. Shake the tray to move the olives around every day. Rinse the olives and then sprinkle them generously with salt. You now need another container – a perforated 2 litre ice-cream container is ideal. Put a layer of olives in the container and then add some fennel seeds, garlic, chilli and dried oregano.

Continue the layers until you run out of olives. Force another container or a flat disc of plastic down inside the container, and weight it with a heavy tin or jar. Every day, remove the weights and stir and then re-cover and replace the weights. Do this for at least a week. Taste after this time and continue for a few more days if the olives are still at all bitter.

Wash the olives in warm water, discarding the flavourings, and dry in a clean cloth. Spread on an oven tray and place in a low oven (160°C) for 5 minutes. Place the olives in a bowl and add more fennel seed, garlic, chilli and dried oregano and a little olive oil. Keep in the refrigerator. Rosa happily stores them in bags in the freezer if she has made a lot.

ABOVE AND OPPOSITE The smooth-shelled swimming scallops (*Amusium balloti*) that we served at our lunch look quite different from those we are accustomed to in the south-eastern states and are deservedly famous in Western Australia.

Grilled scallops with sauce vierge

16 scallops on the half shell
olive oil
$^1/_2$ cup tiny rocket leaves
$^1/_2$ cup tiny spinach leaves

SAUCE
4 tablespoons very fruity extra-virgin olive oil
2 roasted and skinned red capsicums (see page 93),
   cut into 1 cm dice
3 fully ripe red tomatoes, peeled and cut into
   1 cm dice
1 teaspoon chilli paste *or* $^1/_2$ teaspoon finely chopped
   fresh chillies
2 tablespoons coarsely chopped flat-leaf parsley
2 tablespoons coarsely chopped fresh basil
juice of 1 lemon

❧ SERVES 4
Cut each scallop away from the shell and slice away the intestinal thread on the side and

remove any wispy trace of 'beard'. Wipe with a damp cloth but do not wash. Wash the shells very well and dry briefly in a hot oven. Arrange four shells on each of the four serving plates.

Brush the scallops very lightly with olive oil and place them on a flat tray while you heat a chargrill or an overhead grill or a very heavy frying pan. While the grill is heating, divide the small salad leaves between the prepared shells.

To make the sauce. Warm the oil in a small pan and add the capsicum, tomato, chilli, herbs and lemon juice. Swirl to mix and warm through.

When the grill surface is very hot, give it a quick brush with a few drops of oil and sear the scallops. They should develop a rich caramel colour on the edges and hiss most satisfactorily. Turn them over after 30 seconds and cook the other side. Transfer one scallop to each shell and quickly spoon the sauce over them. Serve at once with bread on the table for mopping.

Scallops with black bean sauce

Fermented black beans are widely available, certainly in all Asian stores. They are usually sold dried in cellophane packs or occasionally in liquid in tins. In the latter case, drain and dry very well on paper towels before using.

40 scallops on the half shell
$^1/_2$ teaspoon sugar
1 tablespoon light soy sauce
2 tablespoons rice wine *or* dry sherry
3 tablespoons vegetable oil
2 cm piece ginger, finely sliced
2 cloves garlic, finely sliced
2 spring onions, including half green tops, sliced
1 tablespoon fermented black beans, lightly crushed
$^1/_2$ cup water
4 handfuls tender coriander sprigs

❧ SERVES 4
Prepare the scallops and 12 shells as for the recipe above. Mix together the sugar, soy sauce and rice wine.

Heat a wok until very hot and then add the oil. Add the ginger, garlic, spring onions and black beans, stirring quickly until they become fragrant. Add the scallops and toss and tumble for 1 minute. Add the rice wine mixture, stir, and then add the water. Cover and, keeping the heat high, steam-cook for another minute. Transfer three or four scallops with sauce to each shell and top with sprigs of coriander. Serve at once.

ABOVE In David Backwell's 100-year-old house we planned our trip to New Norcia over a cup of tea, a chicken pasty and a delicious custard tart.

OPPOSITE These bright green salad leaves were among David's contributions to our lunch. His chickens lay excellent eggs and love scratching around in his vegetable garden.

VEGETABLES AND CHICKENS

David | *David Backwell was one of my most talented chefs at Stephanie's Restaurant and worked with me for five years.* Seven years ago he moved to live and work in Perth, looking for a complete break from the pressured life of a restaurant. Soon after his move west, I was intrigued to hear that David had become a baker at the newly revived woodfired bakery at the Benedictine Monastery at New Norcia, 130 kilometres north of Perth. He continued in this job for six months. That was in 1993. We have always stayed in touch and in fact when I had a sudden staffing crisis two years ago David dropped everything, took annual leave and came to my rescue.

At his lovely old house, I noticed that the tangible souvenir of his time as a baker was a creative use of flour bags. Neatly sewn together they made a double-bed cover, cushion covers and even table napkins. As the first baker employed by Kingsley Sullivan, the man responsible for the revival of the bakery at the New Norcia monastery, I knew that David would be good company and a good guide for our visit there.

David may be domesticated but he is hardly conventional. He works from 5.30 in the morning until early afternoon at a hospital. He says he is expected to make a good custard tart, baked bread and butter pudding or something similar if he is 'on sweets'; turn out a splendid tuna mornay if 'on fish'; or make a soup with fresh vegetables and stock. I cannot help being astonished at this turning away from his former preoccupation with culinary adventure, but as David says, he now has plenty of time to pursue other interests, which at present include a bit of house renovating, a lot of gardening, and the care of his large family of chickens.

His vegetable patch includes an asparagus bed, salad plants, potatoes and rows of tomatoes and snowpeas. The garden is well fertilised thanks to the chickens, at present numbering twenty mature birds and pullets with a newly hatched clutch of fluffy yellow chicks. Each chicken has a name and we were introduced to Wendy, who was broody and according to David so intent on sitting on her eggs that she needed to be forcibly lifted from the nest to eat and have a stretch. The other chickens were a mixed family, with some exotics including Rhode Island Reds, a Transylvanian Naked Neck (a variety with fluffy silver-grey feathered legs, looking for all the world as if wearing pyjama pants), and one introduced as a Nothing-in-particular, the daughter of Jesus who became a ginseng soup!

David promised to bring just-picked salad leaves for our lunch and to make a batch of his superb palmier biscuits (see page 36) to accompany the fruity dessert.

Chicken pasties

PASTRY

125 g cream cheese

125 g plain flour

125 g butter

pinch of salt

1 egg for egg wash

FILLING

1 x 1.6 kg roasted chicken, skinned and diced

2 potatoes, peeled, boiled and diced

1 onion, chopped and cooked in butter

1 tablespoon Dijon-style mustard

parsley

2 tablespoons cream

salt

freshly ground black pepper

MAKES 5

To make the pastry. Chop together the cream cheese, flour, butter and salt and push into a dough. Rest the dough for 30 minutes. Preheat the oven to 200°C.

To assemble. Mix the filling ingredients together. Roll out the pastry and cut it into rounds using a saucer as a guide. Place a quantity of the filling in the centre of the dough and pull up the edges. Pinch the edges together very firmly to form a traditional pastry-pleated edge. Chill for 30 minutes. Make an egg wash by lightly beating the egg and adding a pinch of salt. Brush the pasties with egg wash and bake for 20–25 minutes until the pastry is a rich golden brown.

Custard tart

1 egg white, lightly beaten

a little nutmeg *or* allspice (optional)

PASTRY

125 g butter

250 g flour, sifted with a pinch of salt

40 ml water

1 small egg, lightly beaten

FILLING

4 eggs

2 egg yolks

300 ml cream

300 ml milk

120 g sugar

3 bay leaves (fresh, if possible)

To make the pastry. Cut the butter into the flour and salt, mix in the water and egg, push into a dough and knead very slightly. Chill for 30 minutes. Preheat the oven to 220°C.

To make the filling. Beat the eggs and yolks together and set aside. Bring the cream, milk, sugar and bay leaves to the boil and then leave to infuse for about 15 minutes. Pour onto the beaten egg mixture and then strain.

Roll out the pastry and line a 24 cm cake ring. Blind bake for 20 minutes. Brush with the egg white and return to the oven for 5 minutes to set the egg white. Pour in the filling while the pastry shell is still warm.

Lower the oven temperature to 175°C. Grate on nutmeg or allspice if you like, return the tart to the oven and bake for a further 15 minutes or until set.

BELOW   David Backwell's delicious custard tart is on the menu for patients at the hospital where he works.
OPPOSITE   At the Benedictine Monastery at New Norcia, all of the twenty-seven buildings are classified by the National Trust and the town itself is registered on the National Estate.

BENEDICTINE MONASTERY AT NEW NORCIA

It was a beautiful drive to New Norcia. To someone from the east, the bushland was excitingly different, characterised by spiky grass trees, cycad palms, banksias of an altogether different character, and dramatic salmon gums with their bright yellow-gold bark as if lit by sunshine on this very grey day.

One cannot but be intrigued at the existence of Australia's only monastic town set in the middle of the sparsely populated farming country of the Victoria Plains, 130 kilometres north of Perth. Accurately described as looking like a piece of Old Spain, its grand buildings, with towers and church bells, seem to rise out of nowhere as one approaches. New Norcia was established in 1846 by Dom Rosendo Salvado to provide pastoral care for white settlers and as a mission for the Nyungar Aboriginal tribes of the area. This focus continued until the end of the nineteenth century. The next important role of the monastery was in providing secondary education for boys and girls from all over rural Western Australia, which continued until the monastery's schools closed in 1991. Now New Norcia sees itself as entering a new era of offering hospitality to travellers interested in some sort of spiritual retreat or whose interest is in seeing and understanding this important historical site. Sixty thousand visitors pass through the town each year, with more than half also visiting the fascinating museum.

At the start of the twentieth century there were seventy-eight monks at New Norcia. Now it is home to only sixteen, ranging in age from thirty to ninety.

In 1998 the importance of New Norcia was recognised when the federal government awarded the township a grant of $1.8 million under the umbrella of the Centenary of Federation's Culture and Heritage Program to ensure that much-needed additional restoration work could be undertaken. Dom Christopher, the Procurator, points out that although this grant is greatly appreciated, $15 million is a more likely figure for what it will take to fully restore all of the listed buildings at New Norcia. Revenue raising is a serious issue.

In the early years of the twentieth century the monastery was entirely self-sufficient, with its own leather workshop, winery, butcher's shop and flour mill. Other activities undertaken by the monks were beekeeping, baking and olive oil production. Many of the original activities have lapsed but it is the revival of the woodfired oven in the bakery and the continued existence of the olive grove that brought me to New Norcia.

NEW NORCIA OLIVE OIL

The olive trees planted by Bishop Salvado in the 1860s are now probably the oldest olive trees in the state. They are still producing fruit that is pressed to make New Norcia extra-virgin olive oil. The museum at New Norcia displays the silver medal gained by the oil when it was exhibited at the 1908 Franco-British Exhibition. Nowadays the tending of the grove and the making of the olive oil are the special responsibilities of Dom Paulino Gutierrez, one of the four remaining Spanish monks. Dom Paulino is ninety and has lived and worked at New Norcia since 1928. He was the community's baker until 1990. Dom Paulino believes that New Norcia was the only place in Western Australia that grew the wheat, milled the flour, baked the bread and ate it! The community still owns and works an extensive farm.

New Norcia is one of eleven research sites selected by the University of Western Australia to look at different olive oil varieties in order to gather reliable data. Varieties currently being trialled include Kalamata, Manzanillo, Frantoio, Pendulina, Luccino and New Norcia Mission.

I spoke with Dom Paulino in the orchard and we admired the heavy crop on the huge trees. He told me that there had been no fruit at all the previous year but that this year he expected a bumper crop and probably around 1000 litres of oil. His blue eyes twinkled with enthusiasm as he described the traditional methods still in use at New Norcia. After picking, the fruit is transported to the olive shed where it is washed and crushed by two revolving steel-coated cement wheels set into a cement tank. The crusher can handle 200 kilograms of olives in half an hour. A new olive press is being installed in time for this year's harvest.

OPPOSITE AND ABOVE At New Norcia the olives are picked by volunteers, who dislodge the fruit with sticks so that it falls onto hessian bags placed under the trees.

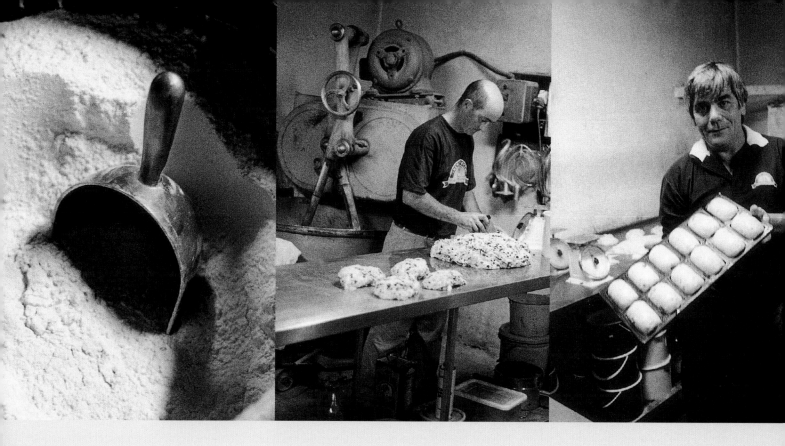

WOODFIRED-OVEN BREAD

Kingsley | *David Backwell met Kingsley soon after arriving in the west and started working at Kingsley and Chrissie Sullivan's Gourmet Grocery in Perth.* The men discovered a mutual passion for breadmaking – especially the challenge of making true sourdough, where the loaves are leavened without any added yeast and develop wonderfully complex flavours. While attempting to persuade the monks to market their olive oil, Kingsley discovered the 120-year-old woodfired oven. The rest is now history! The monks were pleased to have the bakery back in production and it now supplies the daily bread for both the monastic community and the New Norcia township. The first sourdough starter was made from muscat grapes in 1990 and has continued ever since.

The skill in operating one of these huge woodfired ovens is in managing the three variables – the oven at the correct temperature (280°C), the fire satisfactorily burned down, and the bread risen to just the right point when both these other moments have coincided. I watched, fascinated, as the bakers loaded the giant peels with tinned loaves first, then freeform loaves, and then smaller loaves and rolls, and thrust them, firmly but gently, deep into the gaping mouth of the oven. Waves of hot air rolled out as the door was opened. To one side the coals glowed red in the firebox and underneath were the stacked jarrah logs ready for tomorrow.

Kingsley explained that the steam created by the water used to mix the loaves quickly reduces the oven's temperature to about 230°C. When in full production this firing of the oven, loading, baking and unloading is repeated up to six times per night.

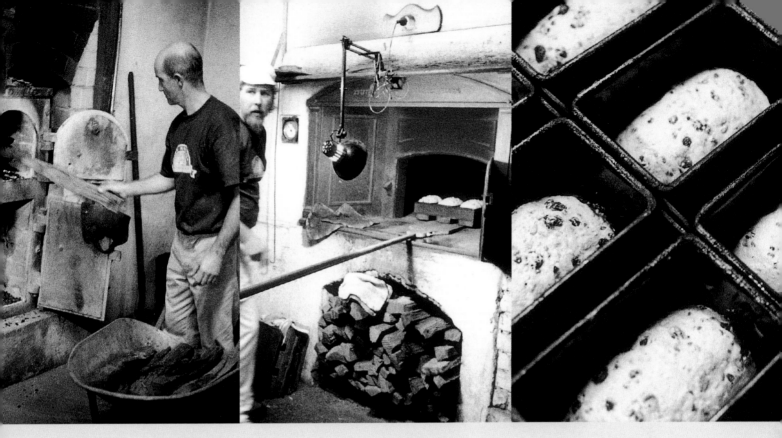

At the end of the morning's baking (which commences at 3 a.m.) Kingsley utilises the dying heat to cook New Norcia Nutbread, a solidly packed disc of fruit, honey and roasted nuts that is a product of this township in exactly the same way as the world-famous panforte is a product of Siena in Italy. David recalled that when he was the baker at New Norcia he also used this slow heat to bake wonderful Christmas cakes.

Today Kingsley prepared a treat for us: a thin strip of unbleached dough flipped and stretched until it was very thin, brushed with New Norcia olive oil, and quickly baked. Once crisp and golden, this pizza bianca was rebrushed with savoury oil, this time infused with rosemary and garlic, and we all rushed to taste a piece. I was reminded of a small trattoria in Rome where this just-baked pizza bianca was the speciality of the house. One ordered it either plain or topped with rocket leaves and prosciutto. The ham was sliced to order for each pizza.

I begged some to take back to Perth, imagining its crisp savoury crust topped with some pickled sardines!

The growth in bread production at New Norcia has been phenomenal. Five hundred loaves of casalinga bread, that is, one-quarter of a tonne, are sold each day, not to mention the other sourdough varieties and the range of yeasted breads. The logistics of baking and transporting these quantities to Perth for sale by early in the morning were just too difficult to sustain and Kingsley has subsequently opened a second bakery at Mount Hawthorn, a Perth suburb, using an eighty-year-old woodfired oven. All the breads are still marketed as New Norcia Natural Bread.

Pizza bianca with herbs

300 ml lukewarm water

10 g fresh yeast *or* 5 g dried yeast

500 g baker's flour

10 g salt

20 ml extra-virgin olive oil

GARNISH

garlic

rosemary *or* basil

extra-virgin olive oil

sea salt (optional)

🐦 MAKES 3

To make the garnish. Roughly chop the garlic and herbs and cover with oil. Set aside to infuse.

Dissolve the yeast in the water for 10 minutes and then mix with all the ingredients other than the garnish. Turn out onto a lightly floured surface and knead vigorously for 10 minutes. The dough should be very light and slightly sticky. Place in a lightly oiled bowl, cover with a damp cloth and leave to rise for 1 hour.

Preheat the oven to 220°C. Divide the dough into three pieces and rest on a lightly floured surface for 15 minutes. Pat and stretch into a long slipper-shape and place on an oiled baking tray. The surface should be dimpled by the action of your fingers on the soft dough. Brush generously with oil and put immediately into the oven. Bake until golden (10–15 minutes). Remove from the oven and brush with the garnish. Scatter with a little sea salt if desired.

Pizza bianca is best served immediately but can be reheated quickly on a hotplate or in a heavy frying pan. It has sufficient oil to reheat without adding more oil.

OPPOSITE AND BELOW   Cut into fingers, Kingsley Sullivan's pizza bianca is the perfect base for Rosa Mendolia's pickled sardines (see page 22).

WINE FROM MARGARET RIVER

Di and Vanya | *It was a special pleasure to meet Di and Vanya Cullen for the first time at our lunch.* I had long read about Di's pioneering role in the winemaking story of the Margaret River region. Di's daughter Vanya is now the winemaker at the winery at Wilyabrup, 270 kilometres south of Perth, and I appreciated them travelling so far to be with us. The wines we were privileged to taste were special and quite delicious.

A wander through the Fremantle Market had resulted in us buying some small and highly perfumed melons, labelled 'Rockies from the Ord River', and some equally fragrant strawberries. We found the 1997 Robinson's Riesling from the Cullen winery ideal with the melon. We cut a lid from each melon and carefully scooped out the seeds (for larger melons, one could halve them and remove the seeds). We poured dessert wine into each melon and chilled them for 1 hour before serving. We added a very festive touch by filling the melons with sliced strawberries just before serving.

Palmier biscuits

It is probably best not to attempt these biscuits unless you have either made the puff pastry yourself or you have bought pastry that has been made with butter. The frozen supermarket variety is not appropriate. Note that the preparation is better done the day before baking.

500 g puff pastry
castor sugar

🍞 MAKES 15–20

Allow the pastry to soften slightly and then roll it out to a square about ½ cm thick. Lift the pastry from the bench and sprinkle sugar liberally and then lay the pastry back down and roll again. Give a final roll to press sugar in and to make the pastry slightly thinner. Roll up from both ends like a scroll, wrap in plastic and rest in the refrigerator for 30 minutes.

Take the scroll and cut into slices about 1 cm thick using a very sharp knife and slicing quickly and cleanly so as not to compress the pastry. Using a palette knife, press these slices into a pile of sugar making them about half their thickness. Make sure they are very well coated in sugar. Lay on a baking sheet and refrigerate for 1 hour or, ideally, overnight. (The sugar dissolves more readily this way, and helps to provide the desired crunchy caramel cover.)

Preheat the oven to 220°C. Cook the palmiers in the hot oven for 15 minutes and then, using the palette knife, flick the biscuits over. Cook for about 2 minutes more. It is important to be attentive at this stage as the caramel colours very quickly. Palmiers should be golden brown and a bit burnt around the edges, I think, for perfection.

A word of caution. Caramel gives the nastiest of burns. These biscuits are *very hot* and the turning *must* be done with a palette knife, never the fingers.

Limoncello

This very popular *digestivo* is easy to make at home. The recipe was given to Vince Garreffa by Massimo Veronesi, a visiting chef from Savona in Italy, where the drink is made with pure spirit or grappa.

6 large lemons (picked from your backyard tree or
    another source guaranteed free of spray or wax)
1 litre unflavoured grappa
1 kg sugar
1 litre water

🍃 MAKES 3 LITRES

Peel fruit extremely thinly, removing only the coloured part of the rind (no pith). The best implement to use is a peeler with a horizontally set blade, often sold as an asparagus peeler. Put the strips of peel into a glass, ceramic or stainless steel container with the alcohol. Cover tightly to prevent anything dropping into it and to prevent evaporation. Leave for 1 week.

Strain, pressing well on the skins, and reserve the rind and the alcohol. In a saucepan, mix the sugar with the water. Tip in the rind and bring to the boil gently, stirring all the time until the sugar is completely dissolved. Allow to cool. Strain and add the citrus-flavoured syrup to the alcohol. Transfer to clean glass bottles (strong enough not to crack in the freezer, such as wine bottles). Seal and store in the freezer at all times. Limoncello looks lovely served in small frosted shot glasses.

OPPOSITE   The small melons from the Ord River were delicious filled with strawberries we bought from Fremantle Market.
RIGHT   Limoncello was a refreshing *digestivo* at lunch, while David Backwell's palmier biscuits were a perfect accompaniment to the small sweet melons.

THE LUNCH

Every dish tasted superb and the meal was most beautifully balanced. The spicy sardine fillets married perfectly with the crisp, oily pizza bianca. The scallops were rich and sang of the sea. Vince carved the veal thickly and the slices fell moist, pale and oozing juice. Elena had been inspired by the last figs of the season at the market and had halved and dried them in the oven for two hours and then incorporated them with the braised vegetables. The touch of sweetness was intriguing. And the salad leaves were so tender and full of flavour. Many of us are offered hydroponically grown salads these days, and Elena and I savoured the opportunity of tasting these plants grown in soil. Gabrielle had matured her individual cabecou cheeses for three weeks for extra flavour. And the delicious dessert wine seeped deep into the flesh of the sweetest melons I have experienced for a long time. Each ingredient had been created, harvested or grown by someone with passion for and a commitment to quality. This is what good food means to me.

BELOW   The table looked sunny and festive set with the beautiful glazed pottery made by Gigi and Cate Cosi at La Maiolica. OPPOSITE, CLOCKWISE FROM BELOW LEFT Stephanie and David Partridge; one of the pretty place settings; Vince Garreffa; Ord River melon with strawberries and palmier biscuit; Jim Mendolia; Vanya Cullen and Lizzie Partridge.

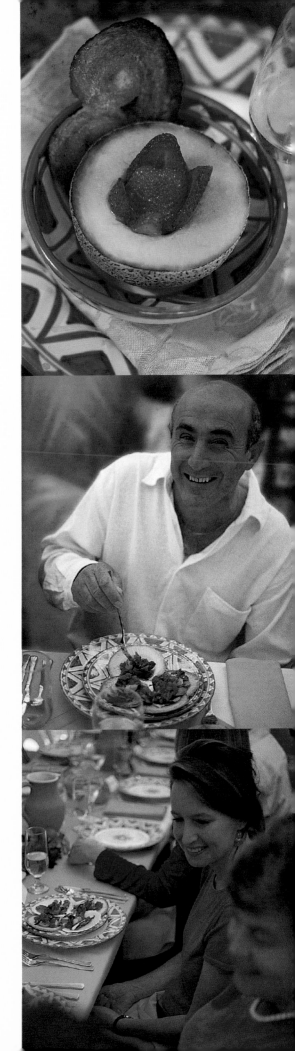

LUNCHEON
MENU

❧

Pickled sardines on
pizza bianca

❧

Grilled saucer scallops
with sauce vierge

❧

Rack of milk-fed veal
with braised fennel,
onions and figs
and crispy potatoes

❧

Green leaves from
David's garden with
cabecou of Kervella
goat's cheese

❧

'Rockies' from the Ord
River with strawberries,
splashed with Cullen
Robinson's Riesling
1997

❧

Wines
Cullen 'Millennium'
Chardonnay 1997
Cullen Cabernet
Sauvignon Merlot 1997

beach

barbecue

Kangaroo Island

I suspect the surprise for me on my first visit to Kangaroo Island, like many mainlanders, was its size. It is Australia's third-largest island after Tasmania and Melville Island. I had no idea that this island was 150 kilometres long and 55 kilometres at its widest point, and nearly eight times the size of Singapore. It was named by the explorer Matthew Flinders in 1802 after he and his crew enjoyed a life-saving meal of kangaroo. The early history of European settlement of the island is one of a wild place visited by sealers, escaped convicts and runaway sailors.

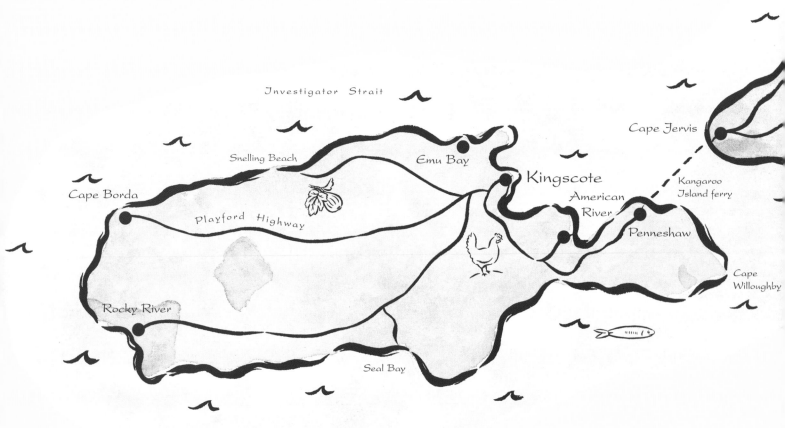

The first official settlement was in 1836 and by the end of the nineteenth century wool-growing was the island's main industry. Later, during the 1950s, it was the site of an extensive land settlement scheme for returned servicemen. The island is still a rural economy but many farmers are turning to new crops or diversifying so that part of their income is linked to the growing tourist industry. The current population is just four thousand.

I was heading for Kangaroo Island via the new fast ferry from Cape Jervis on the tip of the Fleurieu Peninsula. My brother lives in these parts and on the way he wanted me to see the magnificent deserted and wild beaches of the Coorong, only accessible by a trek across steep sandhills up to 200 metres high. He had a gastronomic treat in store for me – Goolwa cockles. I intended to eat these on Kangaroo Island with my hostess, Belinda Hannaford, well known for her appreciative palate and love of the unusual. She was planning a beach party for us and I was looking forward to the cockles as an appetiser. My friends Maggie and Colin Beer were also going to be on the island for a few days and I had invited them to the party. Maggie had promised to bring along a bag of local mussels from American River and Colin was certain to have a bottle of wine under his arm.

PREVIOUS PAGES   The wild, untouched beaches of Kangaroo Island offer visitors superb scenery, swimming and fishing.
OPPOSITE   The Australian sealions at Seal Bay are a popular attraction on the island.
ABOVE   My friend and fellow chef Maggie Beer brought some local mussels for our beach barbecue.

COCKLES FROM THE COORONG

Dingles | *We travelled by ferry from Goolwa, on the Fleurieu Peninsula, to Hind-marsh Island, the home of Dingles Dennis, a cockler and fisherman who agreed to show me how to catch cockles.* Holiday-makers can do the same here in the summer but they have to be sufficiently keen to walk more than a kilometre over the sand dunes. 'They are never called pipis around here,' said Dingles. 'Maybe at Port Lincoln!' (Similar small molluscs are fished at Port Lincoln on the Eyre Peninsula. The Goolwa cockle is longer and more elliptical in shape than the more rounded Port Lincoln cockle, or pipi.)

Cockles were enjoyed by the Ngarrindjeri people, the original inhabitants of the area, who no doubt introduced them to the early settlers. They are regarded by some (mostly visitors) as a regional delicacy and the town of Goolwa holds a Cocklefest in November of each year. Dingles is committed to catching them but considers them only suitable for bait. I tried to convince him otherwise but by his sceptical look I think I failed – even after describing a dish I had enjoyed in France where a plate of similar molluscs, *les praires*, were steamed open and then coated with garlicky buttered breadcrumbs and bubbled under the grill.

More than 90 per cent of the total catch in this area is sold as bait. Recreational angling is big business and the demand for bait is such that cockling is apparently quite a lucrative profession. Dingles has been doing it for twenty years; his associates Alan ('Zapper') and Craig ('Shags') have clocked up twelve and twenty years respectively. Dingles says he divides his time between cockling and fishing for mulloway.

From Hindmarsh Island we bounced across the Mundoo Channel in a small boat to the Younghusband Peninsula in the Coorong National Park. After passing a cluster of fishing shacks we transferred to a rusted and buckled four-wheel-drive truck parked among several equally astonishing vehicles that all looked as if totally abandoned. Zapper and Shags came along to help, and another cockler, Mike Jolley, joined the party, driving his own equally battered truck. We bucked and slid up and over hills of blinding white sand, with much grinding of gears. A few lizards scampered away. We came over one last rise and there was the Southern Ocean in all its magnificence. Spray shot high into the air. The sand stretched away unmarked and gleaming in the sunshine. The surf rolled in as far as the eye could see.

'You can drive for 30 kilometres along this beach,' said Dingles. (Only if one had a four-wheel drive and a lot of knowledge of the tracks through those sandhills, I added mentally.) The beach is officially named Ninety Mile Beach. The Coorong offers 160 kilometres of wetlands to explore and is home to more than 250 bird species. During our visit the weather ranged within minutes from forked lightning, thunderclaps and blue–black clouds to a clear blue sky and burning sun that lasted until well after 5.30 p.m.

The cockler is equipped with a long rake that has a net attached. The method has changed little since the Ngarrindjeri people harvested these shellfish. One first searches for a distinctive rippling in the sand that indicates there are cockles beneath. The feet are worked into the sand to dislodge the cockles. Elena and I agreed that from the rear the guys looked as if they were engaged in some ceremonial dance and Dingles added that the action has been called the 'cockle boogie'. The waves rush in and the rake is positioned, and as the water is dragged out by the retreating wave, the dislodged cockles are caught in the net. They are tipped into a bin and the process is repeated. A cockler expects to spend up to five hours a day in waist-high water, wearing shorts, until the temperature of the water forces him out. The season extends from November to May. During the winter, cockles retreat to deeper water and dig into the sand to stay sheltered until the water warms up.

Dingles gave me a bucketful of cockles and dismissed my plan of covering them with sea water for the trip to Kangaroo Island. 'Better to stress 'em for twenty-four hours if you want to get rid of the sand,' he said. 'Cover 'em with sea water in a day or so and then they'll be gasping and will open wide and release all the sand. They will live for at least forty-eight hours out of the water.'

We had a slight change of plan when the drive shaft dropped out of Dingles' truck on the return journey. Apparently these mechanical stuff-ups are a regular occurrence. No one seemed too fussed. We all transferred to Mike's truck and rattled off again. Then, with my bucket of cockles firmly in hand, we set out for Cape Jervis and the ferry to Kangaroo Island.

OPPOSITE Dingles Dennis maintains that five years of salt and wind can turn a respectable, even if well-used, vehicle into the battered, buckled object his truck now is. ABOVE Doing the 'cockle boogie' on Ninety Mile Beach in the Coorong National Park.

Gratin of cockles

48 cockles (*or* any regional variety of small mollusc)

2 shallots, finely chopped

1 cup dry white wine

TOPPING

1 cup fine breadcrumbs

125 g unsalted butter

3 tablespoons parsley, finely chopped

2 cloves garlic, finely chopped

freshly ground black pepper *or* a little finely chopped
  hot chilli

1 teaspoon Pernod (optional)

🍴 SERVES 4

To prepare the cockles. Leave cockles in a container in a cool place for 12–24 hours, so they are thoroughly 'stressed'. Then cover them generously with sea water or salted water. The shells will open and the shellfish will start searching for food. In doing so any trapped sand floats from the shells. Lift the cockles from the sea water after 1–2 hours, drain and cover again with fresh sea water. Leave for another 1–2 hours, then lift out, rinse with fresh water and drain.

To make the topping. In a bowl or food processor combine all the ingredients until you have a smooth paste.

Take a wide, heavy-based pan that has a lid and heat until very hot. Tip in the shellfish, shallots and wine and jam on the lid. Give pan a shake every 2 minutes. After 6 minutes remove from the heat, lift lid and inspect. The shells will have snapped open and the shellfish are cooked. Discard the liquid or use it in a fish soup or a pasta sauce (such as the linguine recipe on page 50).

Remove the cockles one at a time, discard the top shell and place the half containing the meat on a pan that will hold all the shellfish in one layer and will fit under your grill. Preheat the grill to very hot.

Using a small spoon coat the shellfish with the flavoured butter topping, smoothing it over so the shellfish is completely covered. Place pan in position and grill for several minutes until the topping is bubbling and the crumbs are turning golden and crusty. Serve at once with a basket of bread to mop up the juices.

The method for preparing cockles described in this recipe was given to me by cockler Dingles Dennis. It was outstandingly successful. Never before have I eaten a cockle or pipi that did not harbour a few grains of trapped sand. This dish also works well with small to medium-sized mussels.

OPPOSITE   Pelicans are a familiar sight on the beaches of the Coorong.
BELOW   Elena and I stood inside the rusted shell of what had once been a freezer on the tray of Dingles' truck and held on very tightly as we rode over the dunes to harvest cockles for our beach barbecue.

Cockles and mussels steamed over the campfire

BELOW AND OPPOSITE For the barbecue we steamed our freshly caught cockles and Maggie Beer's mussels over a fire lit inside the inner drum of an old washing machine. Elena made flatbreads, cooked on a campfire hotplate, with which to mop up the juices.

mussels

cockles, 'stressed', soaked and rinsed
  (see page 47)

white wine

finely chopped onion

finely chopped parsley

finely chopped chilli (optional)

Kangaroo Island olive oil

lemon wedges

campfire flatbreads (see page 49)

freshly ground black pepper

Remove the beards of the mussels and rinse thoroughly. Heat a camp oven suspended over the fire. Scatter in the shellfish. Tip in a slosh of white wine and some onion and parsley (chilli, too, if you wish). Replace the lid for about 5 minutes. Lift the lid to check if the shellfish have opened. When ready, remove the camp oven, shake in some olive oil and scoop the contents into a bowl that can be handed around. Have available wedges of lemon, bread for mopping and a large pepper grinder.

Campfire flatbreads

Use these breads to mop up all manner of delicious sauces or as wrappers for barbecued sausages. The delicious Middle Eastern spice mix known as *za'atar* can be sprinkled over before baking. Or grate Kangaroo Island haloumi cheese over the top while the breads are still hot and finish with slices of ripe fig.

½ teaspoon instant dried yeast

175 g wholemeal plain flour

300 ml water

1 teaspoon Kangaroo Island sea salt

2 teaspoons Kangaroo Island olive oil

1 tablespoon garlic, crushed to a paste

1 tablespoon crispy fried shallots (sold in packets at Asian grocers)

200 g unbleached plain flour

extra olive oil for brushing

🌾 MAKES 10

Mix dried yeast with wholemeal flour in a bowl, add water and work to a sloppy smooth mixture using a fork or whisk or an electric beater. Cover with plastic wrap or a tea towel and allow to double and look frothy (about 1 hour). Add the salt, oil, garlic and shallots and then the plain flour. Knead well to make a soft dough. It will be a little sticky. Allow dough to double again (about 1 hour). Turn dough onto a floured board and divide into 10 pieces. Roll each one out to a rough circle about 5 mm thick, and place on a tray or board. Paint very lightly with additional oil to prevent a crust forming. Allow to rest for 10 minutes.

Heat a camp frying pan to moderate and cook each bread for 2 minutes per side. The breads will puff up a little. Keep warm in a folded tea towel until all are cooked.

Cockles with linguine

48 cockles, 'stressed', soaked and rinsed (see page 47)
1 cup dry white wine
2 shallots, finely chopped
5 litres water
1 tablespoon salt
500 g linguine *or* spaghetti
3 tablespoons extra-virgin olive oil
2 cloves garlic, finely chopped
1 cup fresh tomato sauce (use a quality bottled tomato sauce when fresh tomatoes are not ripe and juicy)
1 teaspoon finely grated lemon zest
2 tablespoons fennel leaves, finely chopped
3 tablespoons parsley, finely chopped
sea salt
freshly ground black pepper

SERVES 4

Cook the cockles with the wine and shallots as instructed on page 47. Discard the top shell. (Some cooks prefer to discard both shells, so please yourself.) Strain the liquid in the pan through a very fine strainer and reserve it for the sauce. Place the water and salt in a large pot, bring to the boil and then add the pasta.

Heat the oil, sauté the garlic for 1 minute and then add the tomato sauce and reserved cockle cooking juices. Add the cockles, lemon zest, fennel and parsley and quickly bubble together. Taste for salt. Drain the pasta, return it to the hot pot and drizzle over some additional extra-virgin olive oil. Grind over the pepper and divide between heated serving bowls. Spoon the sauce onto each portion and serve.

Elena's rust-coloured fish soup with cockles

To make croutons, cut a baguette into slices, brush with extra-virgin olive oil and bake in a hot oven for a few minutes until golden. After removing the croutons from the oven swipe them lightly with a cut clove of garlic.

2 red onions, diced
1 clove garlic
1/2 stalk celery, diced
1 small carrot
4 tablespoons extra-virgin olive oil
300–500 g scaled whole fish (such as flathead *or* mulloway), chopped into 2 cm slices
8 tomatoes, peeled and diced
50 ml red wine
approximately 2 litres water
pinch saffron powder
salt and pepper
1 sprig thyme
40 cockles, 'stressed', soaked and rinsed (see page 47)
freshly chopped parsley

SERVES 4–6

Sauté the onion, garlic, celery and carrot in the oil until they are softened and well coloured. Add the fish and fry for 5 minutes. Add the diced tomato and wine. Cover generously with water. Add the saffron, a little salt and pepper and the thyme. Cook at a simmer for 40 minutes.

Pass through the coarse disc of a mouli, pressing very well on the solids. Add the cockles (they will open in the soup). Scatter over plenty of parsley and serve with croutons.

OPPOSITE Evocative sights greet the eye wherever you look on Kangaroo Island. Here, an old boat lies in a dried-out dam.

TETRAGONIA

Mike | *Near the Kangaroo Island ferry terminus we collected some young leaves of the indigenous plant tetragonia.* We were guided to the spot by Mike McKelvey, a research biologist who has lived on the island for a very long time and is passionate about preserving the environment, and about spreading the knowledge that there are good things out there that can be gathered and enjoyed.

When I was growing up on the Mornington Peninsula my mother sometimes picked a green fleshy plant that grew luxuriantly around the base of the tea-trees. She cooked it and we knew it as New Zealand spinach. Later I discovered that it was being marketed as Warrigal greens by those pioneering the bush food industry. Later still I saw it being sold in a posh vegetable market in Paris as *tetragone*. Now I know that it is correctly known as *Tetragonia tetragonioides*. I do not recall the green I ate being as salty as the variety we picked on Kangaroo Island, so maybe it reflects its habitat. The plants of my youth were grown in a seaside town but away from the sea in a light sandy soil, whereas today we have picked within metres of the sea.

Tim Low in *Wild Food Plants of Australia* tells us that the plant was one of Captain Cook's many famous discoveries and that it was eaten by the *Endeavour* crew to allay scurvy. Indigenous to Australia and New Zealand, it is widely found on sandy beaches, in sandy soils and on many a vacant block. Tim Low suggests it can be eaten raw but I find it far too salty and with a quite unpleasant aftertaste. However, once quickly blanched in plenty of boiling water, the leaves turn the brightest green and taste of highly seasoned young green beans. I find no resemblance to the texture or flavour of spinach as is widely claimed.

Tetragonia goes beautifully with fish. Pick the smallest and most tender shoots. Either scatter the cleaned and blanched shoots over cooked fish or drop the shoots in a butter sauce. Alternatively, warm the tetragonia in extra-virgin olive oil and spoon over cooked fish. Do not delay this, as the blanched leaves will turn almost black if left to stand long.

OPPOSITE Tetragonia grows in many different locations. Here, I am gathering it from rocks right on the seashore.
BELOW The island boasts many ideal picnic spots, such as this one near Middle River, behind Snelling Beach.

HANNAFORD'S CLIFF HOUSE

Tourists visiting Kangaroo Island are attracted by its wild beauty and tranquil environment, its stunning beaches, its great fishing, and the ease with which they can experience native animals in the wild. Or perhaps they have heard of Belinda Hannaford's Cliff House on the north coast of the island. Designed as a 'castle on the cliff' and surrounded by rolling hills, this very special retreat overlooks beautiful Snelling Beach near the mouth of Middle River.

Belinda and Prue | *Belinda Hannaford is well known on Kangaroo Island.* And so is her 86-year-old mother, Lady (Prue) Holden. This extraordinary pair know everybody, and take on any challenge with gusto and enthusiasm, including such diverse pursuits as mastering the techniques of wind-powered generators, re-vegetating slopes of cleared land, maintaining a vegetable garden, restoring the habitat of the glossy black red-tailed cockatoo (Kangaroo Island has South Australia's only remaining colony of this species), establishing Landcare groups, and masterminding 'events' for guests who holiday in one of their several properties at Snelling Beach. They both tear around the island attending to things, each in her own four-wheel-drive truck. Belinda's nickname is 'Whirlybird' and her mother's is 'Turbo'. I found both names delightfully apt.

On an earlier visit to the island I had been met by Belinda at night and driven for more than an hour in her much-loved Land Rover. It was a surreal experience: driving through the dark along an endless corrugated road, crowded in by dense bush and watching in fascination as possums, wombats, wallabies and some unknown animals scattered to right and left, seeming miraculously to survive. The noise of the loose stones crashing into the chassis and the roar of the engine made conversation impossible, so I just settled into the experience. On arrival I could see nothing but I could hear the waves sucking and thudding on a beach and the air was salty. Dinner had been in Belinda's own house, even higher up the cliff.

During the meal we had discussed the future of the island. Belinda believes islanders must strive to achieve a balance between tourism, farming and ecology; and take into account the reality around them. In order to effect change the opinions of others must be accommodated. The future of tourism on Kangaroo Island depends on recognising its special quality and ensuring that development does not destroy what it is the visitors come to enjoy. For European visitors especially, Kangaroo Island fulfils many of their expectations of Australia – wildlife, dirt roads, sheep farms, stunning beaches, few people and pleasant weather.

After much talk I had retired to bed. And in the morning I sleepily opened one eye and there in front of me was the furious ocean, foaming and rushing onto a curve of sand framed by a black cliff. I felt as if I was in a lighthouse, or maybe a high-tech cinema with wraparound sound of roaring waves and sighing wind.

On this visit Elena and I arrived in daylight. The sea was a glorious blue. It curled lazily and creamily onto the pristine white sand of Snelling Beach, unmarked by anything other than the prints of seabirds. The cliff was not black but flashed a brilliant orange wherever the sun hit it. The low vegetation was bronze and olive-green. The blue of the sky equalled that of the ocean and there was just the gentlest breeze. It was not difficult to imagine the incredulity of a European visitor looking at this perfect landscape.

Over breakfast I discussed the beach barbecue I had planned with Belinda. She became more and more animated. She loves nothing better than to make it all happen for her delighted guests. All I needed to do now was to find the people who would provide the meal! And she knew just who I should see.

BELOW   Snelling Beach is one of the many glorious and secluded beaches on Kangaroo Island.

Prue's beer cake

This is my version of Prue's tattered recipe card. Her notes list '1/2 bot beer'. I have assumed that the bottle was a 750 ml one and have successfully followed the recipe using the half-bottle quantity. The day I tested the recipe I had no raisins, sultanas or currants, so I substituted 1 cup mixed peel and 1 cup walnut halves. It was still very good.

3 cups self-raising flour
3/4 cup sugar
2 tablespoons butter
2 cups mixed fruit
375 ml beer
1 egg, lightly beaten

STREUSEL TOPPING
1/2 cup sugar
1/2 cup plain flour
60 g butter

Preheat oven to 200°C. Grease a 30 cm × 20 cm rectangular baking dish. Using your fingertips, mix the topping ingredients to a crumbly consistency.

Combine the self-raising flour and sugar in a bowl and rub in the butter with your hands. Add the fruit, beer and egg and mix to pouring consistency. Place in the baking dish and sprinkle streusel on top. Bake for 30 minutes or until cooked (I used a fanforced oven). Cool completely before cutting. This cake is always eaten generously buttered.

FRESH ROCK LOBSTERS

Jim | *Jim Thiselton is a farmer who has diversified to include scuba diving, fishing and farmstay holidays in his portfolio.* After the wool crash of 1989 there were many like him who realised that they had to spread their risks. Jim declares that Kangaroo Island rock lobster is the best in the world. And in his 26-foot (8-metre) catamaran he was able to supply us with the necessary numbers for our barbecue.

On the morning of our party we went to meet Jim's boat, a hessian sack at the ready for the live lobsters. We wasted no time in dispatching these beauties in the kindest way we know – drowning in plenty of cold fresh water. We used a plastic rubbish bin with a lid and it was all over in fifteen minutes without any struggle.

The southern rock lobster, *Jasus edwardsii*, is also commonly known as lobster or crayfish. Australians know what is meant but the terms can be confusing for visitors. In Europe 'lobster' refers to the North Atlantic lobster, which has very distinctive large front claws and is not spiky like our rock lobster. Our spiky variety is known in Europe, especially in Mediterranean waters, by the French name *langouste* ('spiny lobster' in English). The term 'crayfish' causes even more confusion because translated in French (*écrevisse*), it refers to the creature that we know as a yabby!

OPPOSITE   The instructions for the beer cake came from Prue's recipe card, carefully stuck into her collection of old recipes.

BELOW   It was a dramatic and marvellous moment when Jim's boat came into view and he waded ashore with a pair of snapping rock lobsters.

Barbecued rock lobster

If the lobster is to be barbecued whole it is simplest and most humane to kill it by drowning it in a large amount of cold water (or ask your fishmonger to do it for you). Attacking a live rock lobster with a knife or cleaver is too dangerous for home cooks and risks being traumatic for both lobster and knife wielder.

1.2 kg lobster

HERB BUTTER
softened butter
chopped fennel *or* anchovy
few drops lemon juice
freshly ground black pepper *or* chilli to taste

🐚 SERVES 2

To cook the lobster. The tail will retract when barbecued so to keep it straight tie it to something solid before putting it to cook over the hot coals. We used a tent peg as a splint and secured it with fine wire. The average cooking time for an unsplit rock lobster weighing 1.2 kg to 1.5 kg is 15–20 minutes. Our rock lobster was

put directly onto the coals, but one could roast it on a grid over the coals, in which case it may take a little longer. The shells will turn bright red and the flesh will look white, not translucent, when inspected on the underside.

To make the herb butter. Work the softened butter with the fennel or anchovy until well mixed. Sharpen with a few drops of lemon juice and pepper or chilli if you like.

To serve. Brush away any loose ash and split the rock lobster. Extract the head sac and the intestinal tract that runs through the tail meat. The brown soft 'mustard' in the head is much prized by some and adds richness to any accompanying sauce. The meat clings tightly to the shell. For easy eating, cut the tail meat from the shell, slice and return it. Spoon the herb butter over and around – it will ooze deliciously between the slices. (A fancy variation is to punch a hole in the head and force the herb butter in through this hole several times during the barbecuing time.)

OPPOSITE AND ABOVE   Once barbecued and split, our rock lobster was served with herb butter and barbecued corn on the cob. We took it all to the table in an extra-large bamboo steamer basket.

Barbecued corn on the cob

Anyone who has ever grown their own sweetcorn knows that the sweetest corn is picked only minutes before eating. So choose the youngest corn.

1 corn cob per person
a little olive oil
unsalted butter
salt
freshly ground black pepper

Carefully pull back the green husk leaves and strip away and discard all the silky hair. Lightly oil the corn kernels. Dampen the green leaves, fold them back in place and tie with string. Place the corn cobs on hot coals. Turn once or twice. The green leaves will char on the outside but in 15 minutes the corn should be ready. Brush away the charred outside leaves and peel back the inner leaves. Spread the corn with unsalted butter and season to taste. Delicious.

KANGAROO ISLAND OLIVE OIL AND SEA SALT

Sue and Dan | *Sue and Dan Pattingale started their olive orchard with 100 trees five years ago and now have over 2000 trees.* They are producing excellent olive oil and last year they included some fruit from their first plantings, rather than the oil they crushed from 100 per cent feral fruit the previous year. In 1999 they expect to produce olive oil predominantly from their own trees.

Sue and Dan are quick to point out how difficult it has been, particularly to control predators. Galahs ringbark the young trees; cuckoos, currawongs and grasshoppers eat the fruit; and kangaroos, wallabies and sheep eat the bark. That the trees have survived reinforces the couple's belief in the incredible strength and endurance of the olive. They are not the only growers of olive trees but point to the superior condition and size of their trees and put this down to full-time commitment to their dream. Part-time olive growers are not able to care for the trees in the way that the Pattingales can and do. There are some in the fledgling industry who think that putting in an olive grove is a romantic thing to do and that it promises liquid gold. Sue would like them to know that it involves a lot of waiting and maintenance before there is any return at all. Dan adds that he prefers to think of their venture as an orchard because he considers 'grove' to have romantic implications. To those who see it as a quick way to make money his answer is, 'Give me the money and I'll give you some oil'.

The Pattingales have planted six olive varieties and are keeping a close eye on the performance of each. The two Italian varieties they have planted, Frantoio and Corregiola, were both selected for their flavour potential as well as their high-yielding quality. In 1999 Sue and Dan will crush fruit from two-year-old Corregiola trees. They are not interested in table olives, just olives for oil. The demand for their product far outstrips the supply. The oil is crushed in Adelaide using a continuous flow extraction process and is then hand-bottled by Dan and Sue.

The Pattingales are determined to create their own niche in the marketplace. They also are creative and lateral thinkers. Dan is working on a new project to harvest and market the pure sea salt in the island's rockpools. As a keen fisherman he noticed the crust of white salt that forms in the pools as the water evaporates in the summer sun. He pumps sea water from this idyllic coastline into water tankers and transfers it to shallow evaporation ponds. It is then filtered and the remaining evaporation takes place in enclosed tunnels. The process takes a month and is still being improved. Trials are continuing and at the time of writing distribution and packaging are being considered. I am looking forward to this salt product becoming more widely available. Dan would like to market his unrefined salt at a price that would make it more widely acceptable than the imports.

So I now have extra-virgin olive oil for the shellfish and salad and the purest sea salt to bring out the flavour.

ABOVE Dan Pattingale is very proud of the growth rates he has achieved. His two-year-old Corregiola trees will have crushable quantities of fruit this year.

OPPOSITE Dan expects his Kangaroo Island sea salt, evaporated from this pristine sea water, to rival the pure sea salts currently being imported into Australia from France and Italy.

Child's play
tomato salad

4–6 ripe red tomatoes
Kangaroo Island extra-virgin olive oil
Kangaroo Island sea salt
freshly ground black pepper

Cut the tomatoes into slices, wedges or cubes.
Drizzle generously with the oil and leave for
1 hour. Taste for acidity – you will probably
not need any wine vinegar or lemon juice as
tomatoes are quite acidic anyway. Season with
salt and pepper.

For a classic bruschetta, serve on garlic-
rubbed grilled bread. Alternatively, add
paper-thin slices of mild onion or herbs
(as everyone knows, basil is marvellous with
tomatoes). Or add fat black olives. Be generous
with the oil so there is enough to soak your
bread in once all the tomatoes have been eaten.

FRYARS FREE-RANGE EGG FARM

Next on my shopping list was some eggs for a good mayonnaise. By the time we arrived at Fiona and Tom Fryar's egg farm the afternoon shadows were lengthening. Glossy black-feathered hens were out grazing. In the heat of the day the birds tend to rest in the shade of trees on the property. They looked very beautiful but had no fancy name. Instead they are known as SB2s, standing for super browns. The Fryars also have some red-feathered hens called high-sex hens, and these lay brown eggs. Some members of the public are still convinced that brown eggs, the sort that Milly-Molly-Mandy's mother always boiled for Milly-Molly-Mandy's tea, taste better, whereas they are simply the result of selecting brown-egg-laying hens.

Tom and Fiona | *The Fryars have 6000 hens producing 4500 eggs a day, just enough to supply their markets in Adelaide and on Kangaroo Island.* Fiona and Tom guarantee the freshness of the eggs, which are collected the day they are laid. The hens are a picture of contentment – spread out in the blond grass, making soft noises, with their heads down foraging for good things. There are no foxes or rabbits on the island so there is no need to lock the hens away at night, although they do have roosts and nesting boxes. The only fencing on the property is to separate the pullets from the mature birds. The Fryars are anxious to see some legislation that will guarantee the authenticity of any producer's claim to be producing free-range eggs.

I tucked a carton of eggs in my basket, certain that with my bottle of Kangaroo Island extra-virgin olive oil and my bag of Kangaroo Island sea salt, the mayonnaise I would be making would be splendid.

OPPOSITE AND ABOVE   Eggs from Tom and Fiona Fryar's contented hens made beautifully flavoured and gorgeously yellow mayonnaise.

Hand-whisked mayonnaise

3 egg yolks

pinch sea salt

1 tablespoon lemon juice *or* wine vinegar

300 ml olive oil

white pepper *or* Tabasco

🦐 MAKES 2 CUPS

Choose a comfortable basin and rest it on a damp cloth (or between your knees if you are sitting by a campfire) so it cannot slip around. Work the egg yolks with the salt and lemon juice or vinegar for 1 minute until smooth. Gradually beat in the olive oil using a wooden spoon. Add the first few tablespoons one at a time, beating very well after each addition. After a third of the oil has been used, the rest can be added in a thin steady stream (this is easiest to do if you have a helper to pour while you beat). Taste the mayonnaise for acidity and adjust with drops of lemon or vinegar, salt, and pepper or Tabasco.

As we intended to serve this mayonnaise with roasted lobster and grilled fish, we divided the mixture in two and stirred some of the creamy brown 'mustard' from the head of the cooked lobster into one half of the mayonnaise for an exciting variation.

KING GEORGE WHITING

Robert | *Robert Barrett catches King George whiting, without doubt one of the aristocrats of Australian fish.* With its sleek lines and silver body it puts one in mind of an expensive racing car and added to its good looks is the indisputable fact that it is sweet and delicately flavoured. Robert is a 'hookie' as opposed to a 'nettie' and he explained the differences. He uses a hand line with two hooks and fishes in water 20–30 metres deep in the Investigator Strait, while 'netties' trail a net behind the boat. Good 'netties' inevitably catch small species such as garfish but will always release undersized fish; they are not the villains they are sometimes made out to be, according to Robert.

He was uneasy discussing the politics of the industry although he did comment that pollution was killing the seagrass which provides the habitat for the juvenile whiting. The main pollutants are farm run-offs that empty into the sea. The fishery is closed for a couple of months a year when the fish are spawning.

Many professional fishermen will concede that with new technology and bigger boats, the thrill of the chase has diminished. 'Fishing is now more like a job,' said Robert, although he quickly added, 'but it's still better than shearing sheep' (one of his former occupations). Asked whether he catches more or less fish since he bought a bigger boat with better equipment, Robert conceded that it was not as good as twenty years ago. He still catches the same amount of fish (20–30 kilograms a day) so the superior boat and gear have maintained his catch rather than improved it. The fish are transferred immediately to an ice slurry on board the boat, and back on shore Robert sells them to a wholesaler in Kingscote and that is the end of it for him. The fish he had for me were still stiff with rigor mortis, which is an indicator of extreme freshness. After all, these fish had been swimming in the sea only a few hours previously.

BELOW FROM LEFT   The lighthouse at Cape Willoughby, on the eastern tip of Kangaroo Island; some magnificent examples of King George whiting; Robert Barrett cleans and scales his catch while pelicans wait for scraps; fig leaves protect the fish from charring over the hot coals; the whiting is served with blanched tetragonia, butter sauce and a simple salad.

Whiting baked in fig leaves

4 x 250 g whiting
sea salt
freshly ground black pepper
8 slices lemon, each cut in half
4 tablespoons extra-virgin olive oil
4 large fig leaves, stems cut away

SERVES 4

Slit the fish each side of the backbone halfway through at its thickest part and season inside and out. Stick a half-moon of lemon in each slit and rub the fish with half the oil. Paint the pale side of the fig leaves with the remainder of the oil. Settle the fish in the middle of the leaf, and pull up the sides of the leaf. Fold like a parcel if the leaves are big enough; if not, secure the edges with a toothpick.

Place the parcels over the coals and bake for 15–20 minutes, depending on the size of the fish. Turn once. At the end of the cooking time, remove one parcel, undo it and inspect the fish at its thickest point. If cooked, release the leaves and serve at once.

Simplest butter sauce

If you would like to serve this melted lemon butter with the whiting, it can be spooned over the fish while still in its fig-leaf boat.

3 tablespoons water
125 g unsalted butter, cubed
salt and pepper
juice of ½ lemon
chopped fresh herbs if available

Boil the water in a small pan and whisk in the butter a few pieces at a time, raising and lowering the pan from the fire so that the butter remains as an emulsion and is creamy, rather than overheating and turning to oil. When all the butter is whisked in, remove from the heat, season and add lemon and herbs if using. For our beach party we spooned some of the sauce over the blanched tetragonia.

More sophisticated versions of this sauce start with 3 tablespoons of a winy reduction of shallots in white wine, or sometimes red wine, or alternatively a mix of wine and fish stock, and so on.

The whiting recipe is a good example of using what one has. On another occasion the fish might be wrapped in kitchen parchment or vine leaves or even paperbark!

FOR FIG LOVERS

We left Robert and I turned my mind to dessert. It was to be barbecued figs drizzled with honey. The thing about figs is that you either love them or you don't. Fig lovers can think of nothing better than to pluck warm figs from a laden tree and eat them for breakfast just as they are or with yoghurt, with or without a drizzle of honey (both accompaniments are produced on Kangaroo Island). Later in the day figs are a favourite for lunch with the palest raw ham, or even in the afternoon with soft fresh white cheese, especially goat's cheese. And I have enjoyed a crisp pizza crust spread with soft goat curd topped with sliced figs.

Pushed to think further, fig lovers might contemplate making a simple syrup and poaching their figs, which are even better if one has added a good slug of something rich and alcoholic, like a golden dessert wine or cognac – or as we did on Kangaroo Island, a generous slosh of the local honey-based liqueur, Island Sting.

Sliced figs are wonderful layered over a cream-filled tart, or in a freshly baked puff pastry shape (figs and raspberries make a divine combination). They go very well with cream or a good custard. Some fig lovers crave fig jam, and there are interesting ways of preparing dried figs. Fig leaves make ideal containers for campfire cooking (and figs are good barbecued this way). But in the end fig lovers come back to just picking them from the tree and eating them on the spot.

BELOW AND OPPOSITE   Maggie Beer had told me that one could have a picnic actually inside Belinda's fig tree. This 140-year-old tree spreads its limbs, heavy with fruit and giant leaves, over an area the equivalent of a small house. Its Gaudi-like structure twists and undulates, creating 'rooms' big enough for several people to have afternoon tea or indeed for ten people to be seated for lunch! For evening functions it can be strung with tiny lights. Its spreading canopy protects all visitors from rain or sun or blowflies. And it produces wonderful figs, too!

ABOVE Before barbecuing, we cut the stem end of the figs and filled the cavity with Kangaroo Island honey.

HONEY FROM LIGURIAN BEES

In October 1885 ten queen bees were imported to Kangaroo Island from Bologna in the province of Liguria, northern Italy. Since the arrival of the Ligurian honey bee on the island no other strain of honey bee has been introduced and these bees are considered the last remaining pure stock in the world. There are strict controls prohibiting the importation of honey or any honey product to the island. The bees are very efficient honey producers and are very calm, I was told. Honey is flavoured by the various species of gum and other indigenous plants that are favoured by the bees. I tasted blue gum, mallee flower, broom bush and cup gum and decided that mallee flower would do very nicely for our barbecued figs.

Marsala cream

1 tablespoon sweet marsala
1 tablespoon Island Sting *or* brandy *or* whisky
4 tablespoons barbecued-fig juices
600 ml cream

Combine the marsala, spirit and fig juices in a pan and reduce for a minute or so. Allow to cool and then add to the cream and whip together. Serve with cold barbecued figs.

Prue's sticky dried figs

3 kg sugar
3 tablespoons vinegar
3 cups water
3 kg figs

Day one. Place the sugar, vinegar and water in a pan and heat through. Gently poach the figs in the syrup for 1½ hours. Turn off the heat and leave the figs in the syrup.

Day two. Simmer the figs for 1 hour and then allow them to stand in the syrup.

Day three. Simmer for 30 minutes, drain off the syrup and put the figs on wire racks in the air, or in the sun if possible (Prue Holden rests the rack on a chair outside in the sunshine, with the legs standing in basins of water to stop the ants climbing up to the fruit). Reserve all the syrup. You can reboil it and then bottle it for some future use.

Day four. Turn the figs and squeeze gently.

Days five to eight. Leave for 3 or 4 days in the open air. It is prudent to bring the figs in at night in case of rain or a heavy dew.

To store. Flatten the figs, roll in castor sugar and put in jars or airtight tins. They keep for at least a year, and can be eaten just as they are, added to cakes or puddings, or reconstituted in some of the syrup that has been bottled.

For our finale, we prepared figs and honey, wrapped them in fig leaves and barbecued them. But we were so well fed after the shellfish that we did not eat all the figs. The next day at lunch Belinda surprised us by re-presenting the now unwrapped figs with a bowl of marsala cream. Yet another surprise was how well these cold caramelised gooey treats went with another island product, a luscious Kangaroo Island brie.

THE BEACH PARTY

Belinda and I looked on and offered advice as her young helpers, Charlie and Tash, made many trips to the beach with mallee roots, redgum logs, chairs, shovels and various other essential bits and pieces. Gradually the scene took shape. A shallow pit was dug and the fire laid. Nearby were grills and tripods and camp ovens. A secondary fire was constructed inside the inner drum of an old washing machine in which rested a huge steamer with conical lid – perfect for our shellfish.

The guests gathered and glasses were filled. I quickly tipped the shellfish into the boiling steamer and within minutes was scooping the delicious morsels onto a big platter. A lot of slurping and enthusiastic noises were heard. The sun was sinking as Elena and I split the lobsters, unwrapped the whiting and dehusked the corn. We tucked lemons around the platter and made sure that bowls of golden mayonnaise and butter sauce were spread around the table. As the sun slipped away I raised my glass and proposed a toast to Belinda, to Kangaroo Island and to good fellowship.

OVERLEAF Our beach barbecue started outside near the campfire and later moved under cover to the pavilion.
MENU PAGE, CLOCKWISE FROM BELOW LEFT Maggie and I spoon honey into figs; Belinda Hannaford, our host; Belinda's mother, Prue Holden; barbecued corn; the pavilion decorated with fairy lights.

BEACH PARTY
MENU

❦

Cockles and mussels steamed
and served with their juices

❦

Barbecued rock lobster
Whiting baked in fig leaves
Barbecued corn on the cob

❦

Hand-whisked mayonnaise
Simplest butter sauce
Kangaroo Island sea salt

❦

Tetragonia in butter sauce

❦

Campfire flatbreads

❦

Child's play tomato salad

❦

Barbecued figs in
fig leaves with
Ligurian honey

❦

Wines
Nepean Ridge
Chardonnay 1998
Lake Breeze Grenache 1995
Kangaroo Island Trading Co.
Island Sting

a country

cook

Victoria's Western District

George Biron, a country cook, has his cooking school and restaurant, Sunnybrae, at Birregurra, a tiny and very attractive township at the foot of the Otway Ranges, two hours from Melbourne. It has been affectionately described as 'a restaurant in the middle of a paddock'; he prefers to describe it as a restaurant in the centre of a giant garden and larder – the local region. This is an account of just some of the treasures of that region, with special attention given to the bounty drawn from George's magnificent kitchen garden. When the grass is not too high and the weather is just right, George can expect another local resource – freshly shot hare delivered to the door.

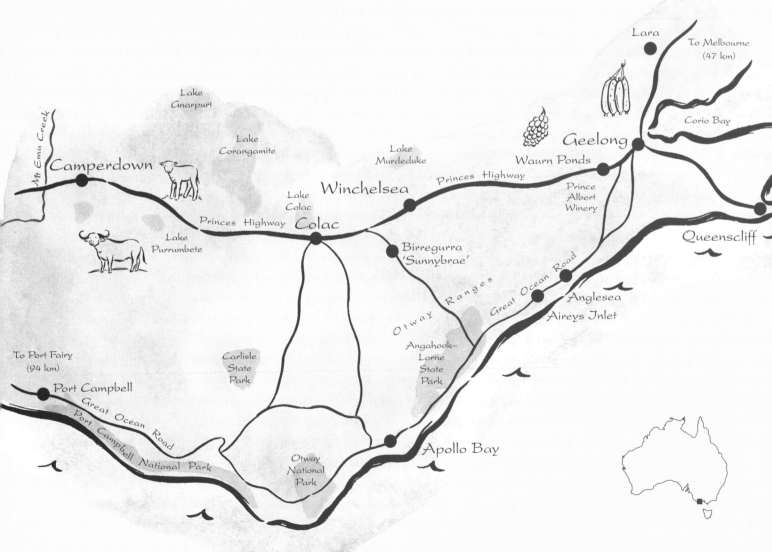

I found myself remembering a fragment from the conversation between Robert Dessaix and travel writer Cees Nooteboom at the 1998 Adelaide Festival. For Nooteboom we live in a sad century and, quoting W. H. Auden, 'the centre doesn't hold', he asked the question: 'How can one keep one's soul upright surrounded as we are by commercialism?'. He believes that the desire for beauty is universal and largely unsatisfied by the mass media, but that the existence of this desire is one reason for the survival of literature.

My desire for beauty is also satisfied by the eternal truths of land and weather and the quiet pleasures that accompany the turning of the seasons. Medieval 'Books of Hours' celebrated annual planting, harvesting and feasting, and despite all the technological changes that are part and parcel of rural life, essentially it is still about preparing the land, planting, harvesting and enjoying the fruits of one's labours, either directly or as income received.

So any contact I have with those who dig and prune and harvest is at once moving and exciting, be they winemakers or potato farmers or prolific home gardeners – such as George Biron. George says that at the height of the growing season more than 50 per cent of the vegetables used in the busy restaurant and cooking school come from the garden, and an antipasto selection such as we planned for our lunch together was a standard offering on every menu at Sunnybrae. The rhythms of the garden largely decide the menu. One grows the food, picks it, trims it and returns the trimmings to the soil, eats the food and then next day uses the leftovers for something just as delicious. An early-morning inspection of the garden is a delightful and necessary part of each day's menu planning.

SUNNYBRAE

George | *George Biron and his partner, Diane Garrett, are living out their dream: a restored 1860s cottage, on 12 hectares of land, extended to include a most attractive and inviting workshop kitchen and the restaurant dining room.* The kitchen window frames are painted a Dresden blue, the wall tiles are white and the floor tiles a rich yellow. The feeling is a blend of a Dutch 'interior' painting and Monet's kitchen at Giverny. I gazed through those windows onto wattles just coming into flower, and beyond to the varied shapes and colours of the vegetable beds. I asked for a guided tour of the garden and what a delight that turned out to be.

With a three-year drought well entrenched and the level of the dam falling lower and lower, it was impossible to ignore the implications of our harsh climate. George had decided to close down some beds until it rained in order to conserve what water he has, but there was still plenty to admire and to gather. Our antipasto was going to be outstanding.

PREVIOUS PAGES The rich grazing land around Sunnybrae had been in drought for three years when we visited.

OPPOSITE George Biron with home-grown produce in his vegetable garden.

ABOVE Quinces are just one of the fruits to which George has ready access at Sunnybrae.

I am certain there are many who have never seen artichokes growing. In the winter these spiky plants grow tall, preparing to produce their main crop in the spring. At the end of the summer the bushes are cut quite low and in George's garden they had produced a final crop of artichokes that were small and tender, with tightly packed leaves – perfect for braising whole. A new sight and taste for most people is the fleshy-leafed purslane plant, here growing riotously, and quite apart from its culinary potential working well as a weed-suppressing ground cover. George uses both the leaves and the stems in salads. Purslane would also be excellent as a vegetable fritter, having both crunch and a suitably substantial structure that would stand up to deep-frying. I saw my first salsify growing. More familiar but rarely seen as lush as this were the rows of purple and green salad leaves, and the glorious gold of thrusting zucchini flowers. We also picked pink and white striped radishes, slender leeks, basil for the tomatoes and lots of wild rocket.

Braised artichokes or leeks

6 artichokes or 12 slender leeks (each about
   as thick as one's thumb)

lemon

50 g butter

1 tablespoon olive oil

1 large onion, very finely chopped

1 clove garlic, lightly crushed

2 cups good stock or half wine/half water
   or half verjuice/half water

salt

freshly ground black pepper

1 bay leaf

herbs to flavour, such as thyme and fennel stalk

orange zest to flavour

freshly chopped parsley

SERVES 6

To prepare the artichokes. Cut through the leaves about halfway from the bottom of the artichoke. Snap off the outside leaves until you reach the pale yellow and rub well with lemon. Using a melon baller, hollow out the artichoke, discarding any purple-tinged leaves and the choke. Do not delay this procedure as the artichoke thus exposed will start to discolour even with its lemon rub.

To prepare the leeks. Cut off most of the green part and discard it (although a little is excellent in a stock). Cut a deep cross in the green tops. Soak the leeks in a deep pan of water for at least 1 hour to float away any trapped dirt. Remove from water, dry well and proceed with recipe.

Heat butter and oil until sizzling. Drop in the onion and sauté for a few minutes. Add the garlic and then the vegetables, turning to coat in the juices. Pour on sufficient of the chosen liquid to come halfway up the vegetables. Season lightly, add flavouring herbs and orange zest, adjust heat to a steady simmer and cover. Cook either on the stovetop or in the oven, depending on space and the amount of attention you can give to the pot. (It takes more care on top of the stove, with checking from time to time to be sure that the liquid is not reducing too fast.)

Once tender, either leave uncovered until ready to serve, or boil rapidly to reduce the juices. Add the parsley or another fresh green herb. I sometimes add a handful of tiny currants or a pinch of saffron or cinnamon to the pan to give a suspicion of the Middle East.

This is a master recipe. Both the artichokes and the leeks are cooked the same way. The length of time they will take depends entirely on the size and age of the vegetables. One thing is certain: braised vegetables are not intended to be undercooked. The trick is to choose the size of the pot with care. Enamelled, cast-iron cookware with a tight-fitting lid is ideal for such dishes. When cooking artichokes it is essential that you use a non-aluminium pot to prevent discolouration and unpleasant metallic flavours. Not a lot of liquid is used and perfection is to have cooked vegetables and reduced cooking juices both at the same time.

OPPOSITE   George cooks his artichokes using herbs, wild onions, a little water and a basic vinaigrette. The acid in the vinegar prevents the artichokes from turning brown. He cooks the leeks with currants soaked in verjuice.

George's stuffing

150 g chopped onion

2 tablespoons olive oil

3 cloves garlic, crushed

5 g chopped sage

50 g currants

shavings of jamon (ham)

300 g yesterday's bread, in very small pieces

300 ml stock

juice from spiced cherries or good raspberry vinegar
   to taste

salt and freshly ground black pepper

SERVES 10

Sauté the onion in the olive oil. Add the garlic, sage, currants and ham shavings. Add the bread pieces, stock and cherry juice or vinegar. Season to taste.

In George's kitchen nothing goes to waste. This is an improvised recipe made to taste using ingredients to hand, ideal to stuff chicken or turkey or serve as a side dish.

White tomato risotto

2 kg ripe tomatoes (not Roma) (makes 1.5 litres
  tomato stock)

water *or* light stock

4 shallots, roughly chopped

2 cloves garlic, crushed

50 ml olive oil

400 g arborio rice

100 g butter

200 g freshly grated Parmigiano-Reggiano

salt and freshly ground black pepper

🦐 SERVES 8

Score the tomato skins and place in a non-reactive, heavy-based pot. Cover the base of the pot with 5 mm of water to stop the tomatoes from catching on the bottom. Heat slowly with the lid on tightly, checking occasionally to make sure the tomatoes have not caught. After about 10 minutes they will be cooking in a clear liquid. Resist the temptation to stir, and let them cook for about 40 minutes at a very gentle simmer. Strain through a very fine sieve taking care not to press or crush the tomatoes – use their weight to allow them to drain (this is not unlike the method for making white wine). The remaining liquid will be a clear broth with an intense tomato flavour. Do not reduce this further as it will alter the flavour and you will lose the freshness of the taste. Set aside.

Dilute the tomato stock by one-third with water or a light chicken or veal stock. Sauté the shallots and garlic in the olive oil until soft but not coloured. Add the rice and heat through. Using a ladle, slowly add the stock in small batches, stirring occasionally until most of the stock is absorbed and the rice is almost cooked. Quickly stir in the butter and the Parmigiano-Reggiano, season to taste, cover and allow to rest for 3 minutes. Stir once more before serving.

At Stephanie's Restaurant we used to make a delicate starter of a lightly boiled bantam egg set in a tomato jelly. It was made by crushing masses of tomatoes and straining the juice, which resulted in a liquid that is stained with just a blush of pink. George uses the same technique to make this delicious and surprising risotto.

It was interesting for me to better understand the cooking of rice for a risotto. George pointed out that using richly concentrated stock as the sole cooking liquid for a risotto defeats the purpose. It may add wonderful flavour, but such a stock lacks the water content needed to actually swell the rice. The risotto risks remaining uncooked. This risotto uses the pure juice of tomatoes as its cooking stock.

Radishes with butter

1 bunch young crisp radishes (allow 6 radishes
  per person)

120 g best-quality unsalted butter, at room
  temperature

sea salt or *fleur de sel*

🦐 SERVES 6

Wash radishes well if pulled from the garden. Discard raggy or yellow leaves. Cut a 1 cm deep cross in the opposite end and soak the radishes for 1 hour in very cold water (which causes them to open out like a flower). Remove, drain and pat dry. Force a little soft butter into the opened end of the radish and refrigerate to firm the butter for at least 15 minutes. Sprinkle with a grain or two of sea salt and bite into the radish. If the radishes are home-grown or very freshly pulled I eat the leaves too. They are deliciously peppery.

Elena's grissini

olive oil

1 whole garlic clove, bruised

fennel seeds *or* poppy seeds *or* dukkah mixture

salt and freshly ground black pepper

DOUGH

250 g unbleached plain flour

¹/₂ teaspoon salt

1 tablespoon instant dried yeast

1 teaspoon olive oil

150 ml water

🍃 MAKES 30

To make the dough. Combine all the dough ingredients and knead well until smooth. Put the dough into a lightly greased bowl, cover with a tea towel and allow it to stand in a draught-free spot until the dough has doubled in size (about 30 minutes). Knock the dough back gently and then allow it to double in size again (about 15 minutes). Meanwhile, preheat the oven to 180°C.

Break off small pieces of dough the size of a walnut and roll each into a thin sausage about 25 cm long. Pour olive oil into a shallow tray, add the garlic clove, the chosen seed or seed mix, salt and pepper and drag each grissini through this mixture. Space well apart on a baking tray. Bake without delay for 10 minutes and then turn. Bake for a further 10–15 minutes until the grissini are golden and crisp.

OPPOSITE   Properly ripe tomatoes were picked to make the white tomato risotto, and the tomato and rocket salad which accompanied it.

RIGHT   I have not seen radishes with butter (above), a French bistro dish, lately. Perhaps even the French are scared of eating so much butter. Elena's grissini (below) were a wonderful part of our antipasto.

Zucchini flower fritters

olive oil

12 zucchini flowers

sea salt

BATTER

250 g plain flour

250 ml soda water

2 egg whites, unbeaten

SERVES 6

To make the batter. Put the flour into a bowl and make a well in the centre. Add the soda water and work the batter until smooth, then mix in the egg whites. The batter is ready to use immediately.

To cook the fritters. Pour olive oil into a large saucepan to a depth of 3 cm. Heat and test to see if a tiny cube of bread browns instantly. Dip each flower in the batter, allow excess to drip back into the bowl and then lower the flower into the hot oil, attempting to keep the petals wide apart to avoid any soggy batter. Fry until golden brown. Drain very well and serve at once, very lightly salted.

George's bread

A television crew has a hearty appetite and George delighted us all with many special dishes. I became addicted to his breads and he agreed to share a few of his secrets.

650 g unbleached baker's flour

350 g rye flour

1 tablespoon dried yeast

1 tablespoon salt

400–600 ml warm water

150 g crispy fried shallots (sold in packets at Asian grocers)

Combine all the ingredients and knead for 10 minutes (note that the dough will always feel a bit sticky as that is the nature of rye flour, so resist adding more flour). Place the dough in a covered bowl and leave in the fridge to rise slowly for 12 hours. At the end of this time, knock down the dough, and work it quickly into your desired loaf shape. Allow the dough to rise a second time in a warm spot until it has doubled in size. Place a shallow dish of water on the lowest rack in your oven and heat the oven to 200°C. Spray the oven with a fine mist of water. Slash the top of the bread and dust with flour. Bake for approximately 30 minutes, spraying the oven with water occasionally, until the loaf tests hollow when rapped on the bottom with your knuckles.

OPPOSITE AND RIGHT   Zucchini flowers are delicious coated in a light batter and shallow-fried until golden brown. They need to be used as soon as possible after picking, as the flowers close within hours. Male flowers (those without fruit) make the most spectacular fritters.

Eggplant with caramelised onion

The caramelised onion and oil keep well in a covered container in the refrigerator for several days. The oil is just as delicious as the onion! If the eggplant fritters are part of a mixed antipasto, allow 1–2 fat slices per person. If they are to be presented as a light lunch dish, allow 4 slices per person. An average eggplant will give 6 fat slices.

eggplant
extra-virgin olive oil
fresh parsley
sea salt

CARAMELISED ONION
20 small or pickling onions, peeled
$^1/_2$ cup olive oil
1 bay leaf
1 sprig rosemary

To make the caramelised onion. Quarter or slice the onions. Tip all ingredients into a heavy-based frying pan and put over moderate heat. (A non-stick pan does a very good job also, but be careful to use a non-scratching implement for stirring.) Cover the pan and cook for 15 minutes, stirring frequently, until the onion has begun to soften. Remove cover and continue to cook, stirring, until the onion has separated and started to turn a rich caramel brown. It does not matter if sections look very dark. This adds flavour. The important thing is to stir frequently to prevent sticking. (If this looks likely, add an extra spoonful or so of oil. The onion can be drained of any excess oil before using.)

To cook the eggplant. The eggplant are fried and should be thoroughly cooked and deeply golden. If the eggplant are very fresh you do not need to salt them. Put about 5 mm extra-virgin olive oil in a frying pan and heat. The pan and oil should be very hot otherwise the eggplant will absorb all the oil. The heat seals the outside of the eggplant and steams the middle. Top with caramelised onion, fresh parsley and a few flakes of sea salt.

RIGHT One of my favourite combinations is eggplant and caramelised onion. Here, it is part of the antipasto, but it can also be served as a light lunch dish with a tomato sauce, or partnered with other grilled vegetables.

OPPOSITE The countryside in this area is crisscrossed with drystone walls built in the nineteenth century. Michael Nocera is well known in the district and the local farmers are delighted by his efforts to rid them of some of the hare which eat the young crops. Michael provided the freshly shot hare which was the centrepiece of our lunch.

Michael | *Michael Nocera appeared as if on cue, handsome, bearded and full of fun.*
He had shot half a dozen hare that evening and told us that 'the cockies', meaning the local farmers, were always delighted to see him. 'The hare eat the young seedlings that have just been planted and bound away laughing. One pair can work over an entire paddock in a night,' he said.

Michael showed George how to skin and gut the hare and we then refrigerated the carcases for a day before starting to make our light stock. I had always found the hind legs of hare too tough to do other than braise, but George assured me that these local hare were young and tender, and that if the muscles of the back legs were cut from the bone and quickly sautéed in butter they were like butter themselves. The hind legs do make a delicious sauce for pasta. *Pappardelle al sugo di lepre* is an Italian classic, and Patience Gray gives a memorable description of a civet of hare in *Honey from a Weed*.

My plan was to roast the saddle, use some of the forequarter sections for a light stock, and use more roasted bones to make the final sauce. I intended to surprise the luncheon guests by slipping in a little very dark chocolate at the last minute to give the sauce a distinctly Spanish or Mexican touch, and also to include some spiced cherries made by George.

Saddle of hare with slow-roasted beetroot

It is more common to find saddles of hare or hare fillets fully trimmed and vacuum-packed than it is to find a hare in pelt, in other words, with skin on and guts intact. A specialist game purveyor may occasionally have a hare in pelt. If so, ask the supplier to skin and gut it for you. You will still need to remove the hind and forelegs and the bony rib cavity to arrive at the fully trimmed saddle. The forelegs and rib section are best used for stockmaking; the hind legs are best used for a slow braise. If the saddles or fillets of hare you buy have no extra bones, substitute 250 g of rabbit forelegs and bony bits that you can buy at the market.

2 saddles of hare (4 fillets still attached to the bone)
2 slices ham fat *or* bacon fat (ask your butcher to supply)
1 teaspoon black peppercorns
½ teaspoon juniper berries
1 teaspoon sea salt
2 tablespoons extra-virgin olive oil

CHOCOLATE AND CHERRY SAUCE
2 onions
2 tablespoons extra-virgin olive oil
1 glass dry red wine
1 small carrot, diced
2 cloves garlic, chopped
½ stick celery, sliced
3 flat mushrooms, thickly sliced
1 bay leaf
1 sprig thyme
2–3 parsley stalks
1 litre good stock (made from some of the forequarter bones)
30 g bitter couverture chocolate, broken into small pieces
handful pickled cherries (if available)

🦅 SERVES 6

Using poultry scissors, cut away any extra bony bits from the saddles and reserve for the sauce. You need neat saddles that will fit into a good heavy-based pan for the searing and roasting. With a sharp and flexible knife strip away all the silver-grey membrane that covers the fillets. Discard it (it is very tough and will also cause the meat to twist in the pan). Place a piece of ham or bacon fat under the belly flaps of each saddle to protect the delicate underfillets. Crush peppercorns and juniper berries using a mortar and pestle or food processor. Add the

salt and olive oil to the crushed berries and, using a pastry brush, brush all the exposed surfaces of the hare with the mixture. Cover with plastic wrap and refrigerate until needed.

The slow-roasted beetroot (see page 88) should be started now, well before roasting the hare saddles. Place it in the oven at 180°C.

To make the sauce. Chop the reserved bony bits from the saddles (and, if you have bought a whole hare, the forelegs and ribcage section). Peel and dice one of the onions. Cut the other onion into quarters. Roast the bones and the unpeeled onion in the oil until they are all a rich brown colour. Remove the bones and onion to a large pot. Tip out any fat from the baking dish and add the red wine. Deglaze over a high heat, stirring continuously, and then add these juices to the pot.

Add all the remaining vegetables and sauté, stirring, for 5–10 minutes over high heat until they have started to colour. Add the herbs and one-third of the stock. Stir well to ensure that any bits that have stuck on the bottom are dislodged. Reduce heat to moderate. Allow to simmer until liquid has reduced by more than half. Add a further one-third of the stock. Again bring to a simmer, stir well, and then simmer until the volume has reduced by half. Add the rest of the stock, lower the heat to permit a very slow simmer and cook for 1 hour.

Strain into a clean pan, pressing very hard on the solids, and leave aside until ready to serve. (Use a metal strainer if possible as you need to press down very hard on the bones in order to bring out their full flavour.)

To cook the hare. Select a suitably heavy pan or baking dish that will hold both saddles neatly and can go straight from the stovetop

to the oven. Heat the pan and seal the hare, meat-side down. Turn from one side to the other so that both fillets of each saddle are browned. Remove the cooked beetroot (see page 88) from the oven and increase the temperature to 225°C.

Transfer the saddles to the hot oven for about 8 minutes. Remove and press with your finger. The fillets should feel firm at the edges but with a softness beneath. Cover the pan with a loose sheet of foil and allow to rest in a warm spot for another 5–10 minutes (while you finish the sauce).

To serve. Discard the ham fat and using a sharp knife cut away the fillets from the bones. Do not ignore the small underfillets on the underside. Slice into thick slices on the diagonal. Chop or cut all the bones into smaller pieces and keep. (They will be useful to intensify a sauce on another occasion.)

Reheat sauce to bubbling and taste it for strength. If it is weak, add in a few bits of the bones from the roasted saddles, cut into suitably small pieces. Simmer together for 5 minutes and then taste again. You need only 2–3 spoonfuls of rich sauce per serve so do not be afraid to reduce it at this stage by a bit of fast boiling. Season to taste. When suitably concentrated, lower the heat, drop in the chocolate pieces, and the pickled cherries if using, and stir until the sauce is smooth. Spoon over or around the sliced meat.

OPPOSITE   The prepared hare fillets are brushed with a paste of roughly crushed juniper and pepper and olive oil.
RIGHT   The cooked, sliced hare is served with George's nokedli (see page 88) to soak up the sauce. Juniper berries are quite soft and crush readily in a mortar.

ABOVE AND OPPOSITE   The small garden-
grown beetroot, such as the ones we picked
from George's garden, are sweeter and
firmer than most of the larger beetroot you
will find in shops. If you are very lucky you
may sometimes find golden beetroot, their
glorious colour reminiscent of a Pierre
Bonnard painting.

Slow-roasted beetroot

This is the marvellous beetroot that accompanies the
saddle of hare (see pages 86–7). It is equally good
on its own as a light meal. If serving the beetroot
hot I would cook them with butter, and if serving cold
I would cook them with oil.

3–4 small beetroot (depending on size) per person
a nut of butter per person *or* enough oil for a
    generous layer on bottom of cooking pan
freshly ground black pepper
sea salt
freshly chopped chives (optional)

Preheat the oven to 180°C. Wash the beetroot
well but do not cut off the root stem or the
beetroot will bleed excessively. Wash the stems
and leaves very well and reserve. Discard any
damaged stems or yellow leaves. Place leaves,
stems and beetroot in a pan with the butter or
oil and seasonings. Cover tightly and put in the
oven. The beetroot should all be tender in
30–45 minutes, depending on their size.

   Slip on a pair of disposable plastic gloves
and remove beetroot one at a time and strip off
the skin. Return the skinned beetroot to the
pan containing the leaves and stems and taste
for seasoning. Keep warm. A scattering of fresh
chives is a good finish.

George's nokedli

George and his family moved from Hungary in
1957 when the Soviet Union decided to 'help' the
Hungarians. Hungarian ingredients and techniques
are still central to many of George's dishes and he
showed me how to make nokedli, a drizzled paste or
noodle, that was marvellous to soak up the rich hare
sauce. On other occasions I have seen George toss
these little shapes with rich paprika-infused stock to
accompany a goulash.

500 g hard bread flour
3 eggs
1 teaspoon salt
water
stock *or* melted butter for resting

🍲 SERVES 10
Combine the flour, eggs and salt in a bowl
and then gradually add water until you have
a smooth paste that just falls off the end of a
wooden spoon. Bring some salted water to
the boil. Into this force small amounts of the
batter quickly through the holes of a perforated
utensil, such as a coarse metal strainer or
colander, using a pastry scraper or the back
of a large spoon. Once the noodles rise to the
top, use a slotted spoon to skim them out of
the boiling water. Refresh under cold water
to rinse off excess starch and then transfer to
stock or melted butter, ready for a quick reheat.
Ideally, the nokedli should be made as close to
serving time as possible.

ABOVE AND OPPOSITE Angel Cardoso's range of smallgoods includes Jamón Serrano hams, salamis, chorizos and *morcilla* (blood sausage). His maturing rooms display sausages hanging in various stages of maturity. It is important to slice salami as close to the time of eating it as possible to preserve its colour and moistness. Fresh figs are an excellent accompaniment.

SPANISH-STYLE SMALLGOODS

Angel | *Angel Cardoso is a Spanish smallgoods manufacturer at Lara, 14 kilometres north-east of Geelong.* He came to Australia in 1962 and like many other food-loving arrivals to this country he missed the flavours of home and set about making them. Settling in Lara in 1969 and an engineer by profession, Angel turned his designing skills to creating a basement area in his new home suitable for the manufacture, curing and maturing of Spanish-style delicacies. Angel has now successfully made and marketed his products for the last twenty years.

A charming enthusiast, Angel loves to talk food and to show off his maturing rooms. I passed down rows and rows of maturing hams, the exposed surfaces rubbed with fresh pork fat. These hams take six months to mature.

Angel is particularly eloquent when discussing the quality of the pigs he needs to make his products. He is only interested in top quality and insists on using female pigs exclusively 'as they are more delicious'. 'If I have to pay more for the product I will pay', he says, and Angel the businessman then adds, 'and of course I will pass on this cost'. He buys his smoked and fresh paprika and aniseed from Spain.

He makes four or five different sausages, which he names after Spanish regions. The one we saw maturing was Salamanca, which is very high in lean pork. Some are spicier than others, but all of Angel's sausages and hams can be expected to lose 50 per cent of their weight during the maturing process. The large slicing sausages will take two months to mature. These costs also must be passed on to the consumer so one can never expect such fine handmade products to be inexpensive.

Angel is enthusiastic about the local climate. In his maturing rooms the air is dry and there is plenty of air flow and the hanging sausages bloom with a soft white mould that smells like the freshest young mushrooms. It is apparently very rare to have this occur naturally and is an indication of a properly controlled atmosphere and of a splendid product.

We discussed his favourite ways with chorizo – the small spicy sausage that is sold both fresh and dried. When fresh it is fried or grilled or barbecued. Once dried it is used as a sandwich filling, or sautéed in slices with roasted red capsicums and potatoes, or in a thick Spanish-style omelette (a tortilla), again with potatoes. Angel admitted that he has reduced the fat content of some of his products in line with what he believes the public prefers. Of course, as he points out, in Spain if one has a ham or a sausage sandwich one would never put butter on the bread. The warmth of the sun would soften the fat fragments in the sliced sausage and provide the moistness and unctuousness for a perfect experience.

As with every small producer I have spoken to for this project, passion and persistence in the face of setbacks have been essential for success. Angel says it has taken him the full twenty years of his business to perfect the ham-curing process. 'It has to come from the heart, it cannot just be about the dollar,' he says.

Angel's tortilla with chorizo

olive oil

1/2 kg potatoes, peeled and chopped into small pieces

1 yellow capsicum, seeds and ribs removed,
   chopped into small pieces

1 large onion, chopped into small pieces

4–6 eggs

about 1/2 dried chorizo, sliced into small pieces

chilli (optional)

salt and pepper to taste

Cover the base of a non-stick frying pan with about 2 cm of oil and heat. Add the potato, capsicum and onion to the pan and semi-cover with a lid to fry and steam the vegetables until they are soft, moving constantly with a wooden spoon to prevent sticking. They will take about

30 minutes to soften. Once cooked, place a strainer over a bowl, tip in the vegetables and drain off the oil. Allow the vegetables to sit in the strainer for 2–3 minutes.

Lightly beat the eggs. Add the cooked vegetables, the sliced chorizo and a little chilli if desired, and mix together. Season.

Heat a tablespoon of oil in the frying pan over a gentle heat. Pour in the egg and vegetable mixture. Once the tortilla is firm, put a plate over the pan and turn the whole thing over. With the tortilla sitting to the side on the plate, add a little more oil to the pan before returning the tortilla to cook the other side. Cook the tortilla 2–3 times each side, although there is no need to add extra oil after the second time.

Most commonly in Spain you will find the plain tortilla: simply eggs, potato and onion. Angel adds his own chorizo and says that although you are unlikely to find it done in Spain, you can also add a little chilli. Chorizo sausage is available fresh or dried from gourmet delicatessens and specialist butchers. The fresh sausage requires either boiling or frying before you can eat it and is not as rich and flavoursome as the dried version, which is obviously given time to mature.

Angel's blood pudding sausage

80 g salt

325 g oats

1 tablespoon cumin

2 teaspoons white pepper

2 teaspoons paprika

2 large onions, chopped

1 litre pig's blood

1.5 kg mix shoulder pork and soft belly fat,
   chopped into small pieces

natural sausage casings in size of your choice

☙ MAKES ABOUT 3 KG OR 20–24 SAUSAGES

The ratio of meat to fat used here is up to
individual taste. Combine the ingredients in a
bowl with your hands or use an electric mixer.
Fill the casings with the mixture. The sausages
can be tied in a horseshoe shape or kept
straight. Put into a pot of cold water, bring to
simmering point and poach gently for about 30
minutes.

I am a great fan of a well-made blood
sausage and Angel was most generous
in handing over his recipe. Pig's blood is
not easy to obtain but not impossible,
and will almost certainly be supplied to
your butcher frozen. Keep it in your
freezer until you are ready to use it and
allow it to thaw at room temperature.
The sausages must then be made
without delay and if not to be eaten
at once are best frozen.

Blood pudding sausage with lentils

2 sweet red capsicums

375 g lentils

1 carrot, diced

1 red onion, diced

1 stick celery, diced

2 fat cloves garlic, diced

bay leaf

hefty sprig thyme

2 blood pudding sausages (see above)

sea salt

freshly ground black pepper

extra-virgin olive oil

small pieces of bread, fried or grilled

☙ SERVES 6

To roast the capsicums. If using an electric
grill or an oven, halve the capsicums and
remove the seeds and white ribs. Brush the
capsicum halves lightly with oil and grill on a
foil-lined tray or roast in a hot oven until the
skin has blackened. If using an open flame (a
gas jet or barbecue), turn a whole capsicum
over the flame until the skin has blackened

evenly. Put the capsicum in a plastic bag or
wrap it in a cloth for at least 10 minutes, when
it will be cool enough to handle. The skin will
slip off quite easily. If there are still a lot of
black specks left, wash your hands and then
wipe the capsicum with a damp cloth. Split
open the whole capsicum and remove the ribs
and seeds. Cut into thick strips.

Rinse the lentils and place them in a pot
with the carrot, onion, celery, garlic and herbs.
Cover with cold water by a good 5 cm,
put on the lid and bring slowly to the boil.
Reduce the heat to a simmer and cook for
10 minutes.

Lift the lid from the lentils, add the sausages
and replace the lid for a further 10 minutes.
Check that the lentils are tender, and add the
roasted capsicum strips. Check for seasoning.
Remove the sausages and cut each one into
three, then return the sausage pieces to the
lentils. Place everything in a serving dish and
finish with a slurp of extra-virgin olive oil.
Garnish with pieces of fried or grilled bread.

OPPOSITE   Angel has several favourite ways
of enjoying blood sausage. Slices can be fried
or grilled and enjoyed on squares of fried
bread as tapas. Best of all is the combination
of a whole blood pudding sausage simmered
with lentils and roasted red capsicums, as
shown here.

OPPOSITE   When we visited Roger at
Purrumbete the whole area was in the grip
of a drought. The dry yellow grass of the
paddocks contrasted with the still-green
vegetation around Lake Purrumbete.
Roger's buffaloes watched us a little warily,
I thought, as we walked around the property.

PURRUMBETE

Roger | *Roger Haldane, the present owner of the homestead at Purrumbete, is a buffalo and alpaca farmer and cheese producer.* The business is a family affair and Roger's daughter Thea is the cheesemaker. Roger is proud of the history attached to the property. The first members of the Manifold family came to the Lake Purrumbete area in 1838. This rich country is volcanic and has several substantial crater lakes. The early Manifolds were aiming for Lake Colac but others had already arrived there, so they continued on to Lake Purrumbete and claimed the land by putting a flock of sheep on it. The plains are now strewn with stones used by the Manifolds and other early farmers in the second half of the nineteenth century to construct the famous and very beautiful drystone walls, which are still one of the most striking features of the landscape. They were built as an attempt to stem the rapidly multiplying rabbit population (imported by Thomas Austin at nearby Winchelsea as sport for the new landed gentry, and released into the wild in 1859) and also as wind barriers. The most famous is the Rabbit Wall, which stands up to 2 metres high and runs for kilometres between Stony Rises and the original Purrumbete property.

Roger showed me the caves dug more than 20 metres into the volcanic cliff face, which were the first dwelling place for the family, who were fearful of the local Aboriginal people. These caves are still intact and the mind boggles at the idea of living in them. The homestead looks onto beautiful Lake Purrumbete, stocked with chinook salmon, trout and redfin. Ducks float peacefully on the lake's surface, maybe aware that this area is a bird sanctuary and that they will not be disturbed.

The main house is surrounded by outbuildings including an intact blacksmith's shop, stables originally intended for the draughthorses, and a bluestone structure that was used as single men's quarters. Other evidence of the homestead's long history is the orchard, still producing quinces, pears and apples from very old trees.

Farcita

The Haldanes are experimenting with a new product which Roger first saw in Sicily: a sheet of mozzarella that can be stuffed with good things, rolled up and sliced for an instant salad. In Italian *farcita* means 'stuffed'. This product is fantastic for quick sandwiches or for laying over lasagne or pizza. The filling can be as varied as you like. Grilled or preserved eggplant would be a great combination with the cheese.

1 sheet buffalo mozzarella
10 slices prosciutto
4 tomatoes, sliced
salt
freshly ground black pepper
2 handfuls washed rocket leaves
good-quality olive oil for drizzling
olives for serving

🍴 SERVES 6 AS A SNACK

Place the sheet of mozzarella on a perfectly clean dry cloth. Lay on it the strips of prosciutto. Over them place the sliced tomatoes. Season with salt and pepper and scatter over the rocket leaves. Roll up from the longest side, using the cloth to assist. Fold the cloth tightly over the roll and refrigerate it for 1 hour. Unwrap and cut into thick slices. Drizzle with best olive oil and serve with olives.

Purrumbete

ABOVE AND OPPOSITE   At the Bonlac factory in Camperdown we watched with great interest as Roger, his son-in-law Andrew and daughter Thea turned the buffalo milk into exquisite smooth balls of mozzarella.

Beneath the house are extensive and magnificent bluestone cellars. Perfect maturing rooms for cheese, one might think, and they would almost certainly be used in this way were this property in Europe, but Roger assures me that no health inspector would permit cheese to be stored in such an area in Australia.

Stainless steel is the order of today's storerooms. My mind started to think of ways around these regulations. Maybe a version of the old meat safe, with stainless steel mesh to facilitate airflow? Roger allowed me to ramble on, but with a smile of amused tolerance. He is far too realistic a farmer to waste time on fanciful thoughts.

We moved on to admire the buffalo, massive beasts with curled horns and sad long-lashed eyes. They have been imported from Italy and Bulgaria and have adapted wonderfully well to life at Purrumbete. These dairy buffalo are cousins to the draught animals that one sees in the north of Australia, but the draught animals are not milked. Buffalo seem to have many advantages when compared with cows, from the point of view of daily care. They require less feed. They are only milked once a day, which is better for the lifestyle of the farmer and, according to Roger, is less stressful for the animal. Buffalo milk contains 30 per cent more calcium than cow's milk and is at least twice as high in butterfat, so less milk is needed to make the cheese. Consequently the dairy requires smaller equipment, which also lowers set-up costs. However, it has not been a cheap exercise getting the initial herd to Australia.

Roger, his wife Suzanne, daughter Thea and son-in-law Andrew are all involved in the business of caring for the animals and transforming the milk into delicate, sweet-smelling mozzarella. They also make buffalo milk yoghurt and a semi-hard cheese they have named Dancing Brolga. The cheesemaking at present takes place at nearby Camperdown, in the Bonlac factory now leased by Robert Manifold

to manufacture his Mount Emu Creek cheeses (see page 99), but the Haldanes are expecting to move into their own factory at Port Fairy during 1999.

Mozzarella is a stretched curd cheese and the actual manufacturing process is fascinating and quite different to other cheesemaking. There was excitement and tension on the factory floor as the curd approached the moment to be worked. The best mozzarella is always made by hand and as the milk varies a little from day to day, as does the ambient temperature, the cheesemaker can never say for certain just exactly how long it will be before the action starts. The small team of three expertly tested and cut the curd, then worked it in a vat of boiling water until the moment arrived for throwing off the water and transferring the smooth curd to another vat of water, where it was expertly shaped and pinched into the smooth balls we all recognise as mozzarella. Each batch uses 150–200 litres of milk.

Mozzarella di bufala is highly prized in Italy and is usually made, bought and eaten on the same day. This state of perfection is not possible at present in Australia. In Melbourne, for example, the cheese is produced three hours away in the country. It is only made once a week and then distributed to the city outlets, which means that consumers are generally not able to eat their cheese the day it is made. There is still much to be done in spreading the word to the general public that this cheese is special and must be eaten fresh! I read a description in a British food magazine by a journalist who had just tasted his first buffalo milk mozzarella. The comment was: 'It is like angels singing and has the taste of milky clouds'. And I would add that it also has a distinct smell of sweet hay. Back at my own Richmond Hill Cafe & Larder we drain the buffalo yoghurt to make labna balls (see page 135) and serve them with a platter of grilled vegetables. It is one of our most popular dishes.

Salad caprese

1 tablespoon tiny capers, preserved in salt

6 basil leaves

120 g fresh buffalo mozzarella, sliced

4 tomatoes, sliced

1/4 cup extra-virgin olive oil

freshly ground black pepper

sea salt

Rinse the capers in warm water and drain. Tear the basil leaves into 2–3 pieces each. Arrange the mozzarella and tomatoes on a platter, topping them with the torn basil. Season with the olive oil and pepper, and check for salt. Scatter the capers over the salad and serve.

MOUNT EMU CREEK DAIRIES

Robert | *At Camperdown I spoke with Robert Manifold, sheep farmer and cheese-maker, a great-grandson of the pioneering family who first settled these stony, volcanic western plains in the late 1830s.* I asked him how he felt his great-grandfather would have reacted if he had known that his great-grandson would be milking sheep. Robert laughed and admitted that his great-grandfather would have been incredulous. Mount Emu Creek Sheep Milk Dairies was established in 1992 by a group of sheep farmers keen to add value to their sheep farming. No longer run as a co-operative, the fledgling industry has battled through its tough early years and now feels a little more certain that it will have a future. After all, Robert reminded me, there are many more sheep milked worldwide than cows.

Robert says with a smile that grim determination has kept him going. The company now produces a wide range of sheep's milk products ranging from yoghurt to aged pecorino. Its best-known products are Mount Emu Creek fetta and Mount Emu Creek cloth-matured cheese, matured for a minimum of nine months. I love the satiny texture and creamy flavour of the fetta cheese with a handful of olives and some good salad leaves and extra-virgin olive oil. And a well-aged Mount Emu Creek cloth-matured cheese is particularly good with dried fruit or quince paste.

One wonders about the boldness of the initial decision to milk sheep when it is revealed that the usual Australian sheep yields a tiny 700 millilitres a day compared with the 2 litres a day of other breeds. There is a successful and developing sheep's milk industry in southern New South Wales using high-yield Awassi sheep but these animals are not available elsewhere. It is only very recently that Mount Emu Creek has implemented a cross-breeding program between East Friesian sheep and Romney Marsh ewes, which will hopefully yield the larger amount. To buy sheep's milk from other farmers is seen as a non-economic proposition, adding impossible-to-cover costs.

The biggest challenge is marketing the sheep's milk cheeses to a population largely unfamiliar with the notion and with the cheese. There is also competition from imported products, especially imported fetta, that are produced with various degrees of government assistance, and frequently using mixed milk. These products have been well accepted for some time by our Greek and Turkish populations and they are much cheaper than the local speciality product, which is produced with an obsessive regard to purity and quality. As with buffalo milk, ewe's milk has natural advantages over cow's milk. It has 90 per cent more calcium and 70 per cent more protein as it is so concentrated. It is higher in most vitamins and minerals and is very easy to digest.

The niche market is tiny and the challenge has been to produce enough but not too much. The costs of maintaining a factory that only operates part-time are also frightening. Maybe the future is in building stocks of matured cheeses that do not lose value and that can absorb excess milk in times of maximum production?

OPPOSITE   The classic salad caprese is hard to beat as a way of appreciating the delicacy of buffalo mozzarella. With home-grown sun-ripened tomatoes and basil, mozzarella one or two days old and a fruity olive oil, there is little room for 'improvements'.

ABOVE   Robert Manifold is quietly confident that the making of high-quality ewe's milk cheese has a great future in this corner of Victoria.

At our lunch we ate a Mount Emu Creek cloth-matured cheese that had matured for almost two years (since 29 March 1997). It was labelled Vat 1, No 13 and the cheesemaker was John Staaks. Once broached, the cheese inside the cloth covering was a fine example of a ewe's milk cheese, with the distinctive fine and smooth texture, an almost pearly lustre, and a flavour which in this case was well developed.

I was interested in whether Robert intended to sell milk-fed lambs as a by-product of the industry. For the moment he has decided against this, preferring to hand-rear the lambs (using cow's milk) until they can be put out to pasture and grown to become prime lamb. From a restaurateur's point of view I am sad, but I know that the abattoirs are not sympathetic to handling the tiny animals and that buying whole lambs does pose certain problems for small restaurants particularly (for example, space to hang them, expertise to break them down, what to do with the lesser cuts, and how to make the costs work when labour costs are calculated on top of the unit price of one of these 6 or 8 kilogram dressed lambs). But Robert was quick to point out that if he can be convinced there is a consistent market he would be happy to change his mind.

OPPOSITE   On the day of our lunch Robert Manifold arrived with an interesting cloth-matured cheese covered in a dramatic natural orange mould. The colour of the mould can change as the humidity or temperature changes in the maturing rooms. George had picked almonds from a neighbouring tree. Still moist within their green coats, they were lovely with the cheese.

BELOW   At milking time there is a great deal of baaing and bleating. Sixteen sheep are able to be milked at once in specially designed stalls. The weaned lambs are fed cow's milk as a substitute for mother's milk.

Fetta with wild rocket

The wild rocket from George's garden was a delightful surprise. It has all the virtues (more of them, actually) and none of the disadvantages of the commercially sold variety. Its slender leaflets were a soft grey–green and easily stripped from each central stem. It was soft to touch, tender in the mouth and yet hardy. The commercial varieties always need time-consuming sorting for insect damage, yellow leaves and the giant leaves that are too hot and unacceptably tough.

300 g sheep's milk fetta

3 handfuls wild rocket leaves *or* tender purslane leaves

freshly ground black pepper

3 tablespoons fruity extra-virgin olive oil

Cut the fetta into 2 cm cubes and dry briefly on a paper towel. Check the rocket and strip the leaves from the stalks. Toss all the ingredients together at the very last moment. Spoon onto a flat dish and serve at once.

Ewe's milk dumplings

At Richmond Hill Cafe & Larder we use ewe's milk ricotta to create these delicious dumplings. They make a flavoursome luncheon dish.

2 tablespoons unsalted butter

1 bunch sage, leaves picked from the stems
   or 40 garden-picked sage leaves

700 g ewe's milk ricotta

8 egg yolks

3 cups freshly grated parmesan

1$\frac{1}{2}$ teaspoons grated lemon zest

1 cup cooked spinach leaves, squeezed and
   finely chopped

cayenne pepper

freshly grated nutmeg

sea salt

freshly ground black pepper

4 tablespoons plain flour

butter

fresh sage leaves

browned butter for saucing

MAKES 16 DUMPLINGS

Melt half the butter in a non-stick frying pan and drop in the sage leaves. Over a moderate heat and using a slotted spoon, keep the leaves turning until they are crisp. Lift them out quickly, drain on kitchen paper and keep in a warm place.

To make the dumplings. Combine the ricotta, egg yolks, parmesan and lemon zest in a bowl. Stir in the spinach and seasonings. Add the flour and mix gently but thoroughly. Taste for seasoning.

Have ready a wide pan of barely simmering lightly salted water. Form the mixture into balls and drop into the water. Poach until the dumplings rise to the surface. Remove with a wide skimmer or slotted spoon. Allow to drain for a moment and then transfer to a hot buttered dish until all dumplings are poached. Sauce with sizzling browned butter and sage leaves previously crisped in a little more butter.

OPPOSITE   The wild rocket from the Sunnybrae garden was peppery and invigorating, perfect with a sheep's milk fetta.

THE PERFECT SPONGE CAKE

While driving back from Birregurra we indulged in a very rural treat – afternoon tea. The passionfruit sponge I bought from a local shop was memorable, and started me reminiscing. When I was about twelve years of age and taking classes in cookery in Year 8 (or Form 2 as it was then) – probably the only year of my life I have ever had formal practical cooking classes – I recall that the formula for a sponge cake was 4 eggs, 4 ounces of self-raising flour and 4 ounces of plain flour (baked in two 8 inch sponge tins). And we had to take sixpence for the cake box in which to take our baked cake home. My memory says that it was quite a good sponge.

Jackie's Mum's sponge cake

There is nothing like a hunt for a cake recipe to bring a response. Over the years I have twice asked for readers' help and both times have been overwhelmed. This time a friend who taste-tested a passionfruit beauty is convinced that she has the secret.

It is absolutely essential that the tins used are the correct size. My first two attempts at baking this cake were disastrous – the tins were too small and I had mixture spilling all over the oven. This cake rises in the tin in a spectacular fashion!

³/₄ cup (115 g) cornflour
1 tablespoon custard powder
1 teaspoon cream of tartar
¹/₂ teaspoon bicarbonate of soda
4 eggs, separated
³/₄ cup (170 g) castor sugar

PASSIONFRUIT 'ICING'
juice and pulp of 1 passionfruit
cream
icing sugar (optional)

🐚 MAKES 16 SLICES
Preheat oven to 180°C. (I used a fanforced convection oven.) Butter 2 × 22 cm cake tins (minimum 5 cm deep) and line with baking paper.

Sieve all dry ingredients, except sugar, twice. Beat the egg whites and sugar in an electric mixer until thick and meringue-like. Beat in the egg yolks one by one. Fold in the dry ingredients gently but thoroughly. Divide the mixture between the tins and place on the same shelf in the middle of the oven. Bake for 20 minutes or until the cake feels springy when touched lightly in the centre. Remove and cool for a minute on a cake rack and then slip the cakes out of the tins and peel off the paper. Cool completely and then split and sandwich with whipped cream.

To make the 'icing'. Mix the passionfruit juice and pulp with a small amount of cream. Sweeten with icing sugar if you like and spread over the top of the sponge.

The texture of this sponge is best if the cake is made, creamed and eaten on the same day. I find there is too much cake if you use both cakes sandwiched together, so you could either halve this recipe to make one cake, or bake the whole quantity and know that you have enough to serve 16 slices.

RIGHT AND OPPOSITE   The common passionfruit (*Passiflora edulis*) grows easily in Australia and we tend to take it for granted. In Europe and North America it is considered a delicacy and is expensive to buy. A small amount of fresh passionfruit folded into whipped cream adds a delectable perfumed tang to a pavlova, sponge cake or tart.

MULBERRIES

Mulberry trees grow in old gardens and occasionally in public parks. Recently a taxi driver told me of a stand of seven prolific trees in a Melbourne suburban park. I have yet to find them but I shall certainly go and have a look. The fruit is unequalled for staining hands and clothes, which is why one rarely sees mulberries for sale; it also falls when ripe so is often gathered from under the tree. It ferments quickly, like raspberries, so be on your guard as one 'off' berry will ruin the pleasure. Use the best cream and maybe a shaker of fine castor sugar, or even castor sugar infused with a leaf of rose geranium.

OPPOSITE   Ripe mulberries (*Morus nigra*) have a unique rich, winey flavour. They spoil fast, so eat them as soon as possible.

Mulberry fool

If you should tire of eating fresh mulberries and cream, and would prefer something a bit fancier, you will enjoy this mulberry fool. It is just as delicious made with raspberries, blackberries or loganberries, or a mixture of each.

1¹/₂ cups fruit
pure icing sugar to taste (try 2 tablespoons)
1 cup cream, firmly whipped

Crush fruit lightly with a fork (do not use a food processor or you will have berry sauce). Sieve icing sugar over and gently fold in the cream. I prefer the look of purple or crimson swirls in the cream but you can fold to an even colour if you wish. Spoon into small glasses and serve cold but not icy-cold. A simple crunchy biscuit goes well, such as almond bread, or more indulgently, a buttery, sugary biscuit.

Honey wafers with mulberries

150 g softened unsalted butter
240 g castor sugar
6 tablespoons full-flavoured honey
120 g plain flour, sifted
1 teaspoon ground ginger
2 egg whites
500 g mulberries
2 cups cream, firmly whipped
icing sugar

SERVES 8

Preheat the oven to 180°C. In a food processor, cream the butter and sugar. Add the honey, flour, ginger and egg whites and blend to a

spreadable consistency. Spread the batter onto baking trays lined with baking paper to form 8 cm rounds (you need 24 wafers in all). Bake for 7–8 minutes until golden brown. Cool the wafers for 1 minute and then, using a flexible spatula, lift them onto a wire rack to cool.

To serve. Mix the mulberries with the cream, crushing the berries a little to stain the cream pink. Anchor a cold wafer to each plate with a tiny dob of cream. Pile on a spoonful of mulberries and cream, balance another wafer on top, pile on a second spoonful of cream and top with a third wafer biscuit. Dust with icing sugar.

This recipe is from *The Cook's Companion*, although in that book the main ingredient was raspberries. The fragile honey wafers can be stored in an airtight container for up to 3 days. Excess batter will store well, covered, in the refrigerator for several days.

ABOVE   We visited the Otway region just a few weeks before vintage, when the grape bunches were hanging richly coloured on the vines.

OPPOSITE, CLOCKWISE FROM BOTTOM LEFT Angel Cardoso; Diane Garrett; Stephanie and George; Elena; a plate of antipasto; Robert Manifold.

PRINCE ALBERT WINERY

I enjoyed a stimulating conversation with Bruce Hyett, owner and winemaker at Prince Albert Winery at Waurn Ponds, and I eagerly anticipated matching his superbly crafted pinot noir with the dish of local hare. This winery has a venerable history, having been first established in 1857 by Swiss emigrant David Pettavel. It suffered the fate of all local vineyards after the phylloxera outbreak in the 1870s and the vines and the vineyard equipment were burnt in 1882.

Bruce and Sue | *Bruce and Sue Hyett seem quietly content with life.* Their winery produces a pinot noir widely considered one of the best in the country, with full Burgundian flavour and a softness and roundness that distinguishes it from the style of many other pinots produced in Australia. The Hyetts are admirers of the great wines of Burgundy and point to similarities in soil structure and climate between their vineyard and those they have examined in Burgundy. Pinot noir is the only style of wine they make and they cannot satisfy the demand.

The Hyetts first planted their vines in 1975. Bruce has been strongly influenced by the work of Alex Podolinsky at Powelltown in Victoria, himself a disciple of Rudolf Steiner. In 1988 the Hyetts adopted Steiner's biodynamic principles and applied them in their vineyard. Essentially Steiner's belief is that to produce healthy crops one must create healthy soil, free of poisons. Accordingly, spraying has been restricted to copper and sulphur and an annual spray with a biodynamic product, 500, produced from cow manure. Weeds are seared with a flame-thrower, not poisoned, and the vines themselves are watched as closely as one watches one's children grow and develop. Prince Albert Winery is a certified organic winery. Bruce remarks with no noticeable change of expression that many of his fellow vignerons consider his ideas bizarre. I would imagine that the quality of the wine should silence the critics.

Bruce admits to being a loner who is clearly drawn to the reflective and meditative, although Sue hastens to add that they lead a marvellously full life with their friends. Bruce would like drinkers to look deeply into their wine for two minutes before smelling or sipping – to sense the sunshine and the rain and the damp soil that have all contributed to this wonderful product. As I had hoped, the 1992 Prince Albert Pinot Noir proved a perfect wine to savour with the hare.

THE LUNCHEON

By the time the guests had finished the colourful antipasto, they were animatedly sharing their experiences of small-scale manufacturing. Passion and enthusiasm filled every speech. There were also appreciative comments for the food and the wine as we moved on to the more robust flavours of the hare with its magnificent sauce, the splendid cheese and finally to the very special treat of locally picked mulberries. The luncheon continued well into the afternoon.

LUNCHEON
MENU

❧

Antipasto
Braised artichokes with
wild onions
Braised leeks with currants
Eggplant with
caramelised onion
Salad caprese
Angel's ham and salami
with figs
Radishes with butter
Fetta with wild rocket
Zucchini flower fritters
Elena's grissini

❧

Saddle of hare with
chocolate and cherry sauce
served with
slow-roasted beetroot
and George's nokedli

❧

Cloth-matured
Mount Emu Creek cheese
with fresh almonds

❧

Honey wafers with
mulberries

❧

Wine
Prince Albert Pinot Noir
1992

family and

friends

Melbourne

Living in Melbourne suits me very well. My closest friends are here, my children are nearby, and like most Melburnians I have plenty of personal space, in my case a large 100-year-old house with a well-established and much-loved garden. In a few minutes I can be in the centre of the city with all the bustle of up-to-the-minute commerce. In as few minutes I can be in parkland. Traffic and transport and all the business of city living are manageable. I feel safe. My neighbours and those I meet out walking always have a smile and a greeting. I have all the latest distractions when I want them: theatre, music, cinema and exhibitions. And most importantly, Melbourne offers easy and affordable access to some of the freshest and most diverse food in the world.

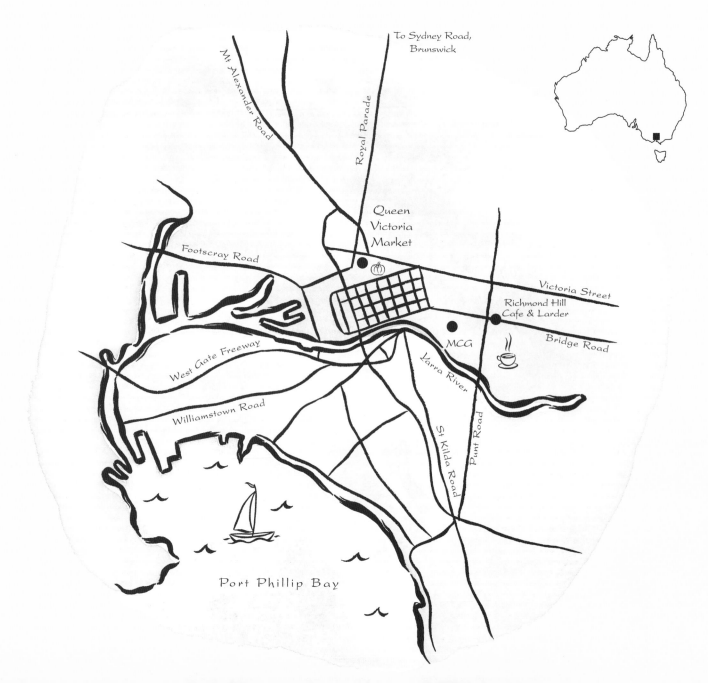

Melbourne's population, like that throughout Australia, reflects our history of large-scale migration. One in four was either born elsewhere or has parents who were born elsewhere. Throughout my growing-up years and continuing to this day, food supply reflected and reflects the preferences and traditions of our migrants. In the immediate post-Second World War years the first 'New Australians', as they were then known, included those from invaded Baltic countries and Jewish refugees from various parts of Eastern Europe and Germany. Soon afterwards came large numbers of Italian and Greek migrants, as well as even larger numbers of British migrants. Among the new arrivals were some who quickly started to grow the foods they were accustomed to, and others who established importing businesses to ensure supplies of culinary staples.

For those who were interested (and my mother was exceedingly interested) it became possible to experiment with unusual pickles, rye bread, unknown cheeses and olive oil. In the suburbs and some country towns we discovered broccoli, globe artichokes and zucchini, rather than the more ubiquitous giant vegetable marrows (although they were pretty good too when simmered with dill and parsley).

Melbourne is a medium-sized city of three million inhabitants, and this number includes the population of our very spread-out suburbs. Increasingly suburbs and neighbourhoods are developing their own personalities, like villages, and their residents are often very loyal. It would be foolish to suggest that some are not more affluent than others but, by and large, the food supply is egalitarian. Almost

PREVIOUS PAGES   Close to the city, the Fitzroy Gardens are delightful no matter the season, and are popular with locals and tourists alike.

BELOW   Almost every Melbourne suburb has a speciality baker's shop – often more than one. The variety of breads available reflects the ethnic mix that is part of the city's vibrant food culture.

every shopping strip has a quality 'gourmet' shop of some sort, and supermarkets increasingly stock items that would once have been thought too exotic. Local shopping centres still generally include a fruit and vegetable shop of the old-fashioned variety, where one either handles the food oneself or is served, but where pre-packaged plastic-wrapped trays of produce are rarely seen. Fresh coriander, fresh ginger, snowpeas, mixed salad leaves and tropical fruit are everyday purchases and the range and variety is continuing to expand. These same shopping strips almost always have a friendly butcher, but less often a fresh fish shop. Large ranges of Asian flavourings and noodles and fresh vegetables are mainstream, reflecting more recent immigration patterns.

One of the exciting things for a Melbourne food lover is to discover the special character of different neighbourhoods. During the city's marvellous Food and Wine Festival, held in March of each year, one of the popular attractions is the possibility of exploring the food streets, guided by someone who knows them well and can explain the mysteries of such delights as pomegranate syrup, smoked pork bones and dried beancurd skin, or identify a durian. Among these interesting precincts are Victoria Street, Abbotsford, for Vietnamese specialities (or Footscray Market); China-town in Little Bourke Street; Sydney Road, Brunswick, for Middle Eastern and North African delicacies; Johnston Street, Collingwood, for Portuguese products and Spanish hams, sausages and much more; Carlisle Street, Balaclava, for freshly made bagels; nearby Acland Street, St Kilda, for borscht, cabbage rolls and extraordinary cakes; and Lygon Street and surrounding streets, Carlton, for all things Italian.

This is merely scratching the surface of this wonderful food city. We have neighbourhood cafes and restaurants demonstrating infinite diversity, we have splendid bakeries, tea houses, serious coffee houses, kiosks at the ends of piers and jetties, coffee shops in art galleries and public spaces, picnic tables in our splendid parks, and last but not least, we have enviable fresh food markets, large and small. I have been an enthusiastic food lover all my life and I have experienced only a fraction of what this city has to offer.

THE HAWKERS' MARKET

The Melbourne Food and Wine Festival in March is a compelling reason to visit the city. Now in its seventh year, it offers something for everyone. One of the most popular events is the Hawkers' Market, modelled on the night food markets many of us have experienced in Asian cities.

The Hawkers' Market is set up in one of the sheds of the Queen Victoria Market and by early morning the space must once again be transformed into its more pedestrian purpose of selling fruit and vegetables. More than 9000 people visit over the three nights. The appeal is the avenue of stalls, manned by smiling chefs equipped with smouldering braziers, barbecues and fiery wok burners, dispensing savoury portions of an extraordinary mix of delicacies. The stallholders are mostly from the Asian community and Indian, Thai, Japanese, Cantonese and Vietnamese specialities exist side by side. The smells are marvellous and the excitement considerable. Some of Melbourne's best-known Asian restaurants participate and the food is of a very high quality.

Tony | *My friend Tony Tan is well known in Melbourne for his culinary tours, and as a television presenter, food critic, talented cook and great eater.* I was looking forward to his company, knowing he would unerringly select the tastiest titbits. And he did. We tasted kid cooked in ginger and garlic curry sauce from Kathmandu Cottage, gado-gado from the Nudel Bar, and butter chicken from Tandoori Den. This was the first round. We then went back for Peking duck from Red Emperor, reef cod cooked with ginger flower from Near East, and a salad of mushrooms and green papaya and a black sticky rice pudding from the Isthmus of Kra. Further meanderings yielded sticky rice and pork parcels wrapped and steamed in lotus leaves, and a delicate green pandanus-steamed custard. And then we sighed with satisfaction. The portions were quite small!

Vegetarian green papaya and mushroom salad

(The Isthmus of Kra restaurant)

250 g green papaya

$^1/_2$ teaspoon salt

1 tablespoon raw sugar

15 ml olive oil

$^1/_2$ cup Thai basil

100 g abalone mushrooms

100 g button mushrooms

4 cup-shaped purple radicchio leaves

TAMARIND DRESSING

40 g tamarind pulp

$^1/_2$ cup hot water

$^1/_2$ cup pure palm sugar

$^1/_2$ teaspoon salt

3 coriander roots, finely sliced

$^1/_2$ cup crushed roasted peanuts

1 bird's-eye chilli, finely sliced

🔊 SERVES 4

Skin the green papaya, discard the pips and shred into fine strips. Add the salt and sugar to pickle the fruit, and allow to sit for 30 minutes. Wash, drain and then set aside. Heat the oil in a wok, add the basil and stir-fry until just cooked. Remove. Reheat the wok with a little extra oil. Sauté the mushrooms for 3–4 minutes. Remove.

To make the dressing. Soak the tamarind pulp in the hot water for 30 minutes, then press through a strainer and reserve $^1/_3$ cup of the water. Place this tamarind water in a pan over heat and then add the palm sugar and salt. Reduce the liquid to a light syrup, cool and add the coriander root, crushed peanuts and chilli.

Mix the papaya and mushrooms well with the dressing. Pile the salad into the radicchio cups to form nice peaks, and serve.

OPPOSITE   A chef at the Hawkers' Market makes fresh noodles – a most spectacular performance.

ABOVE   The effervescent Tony Tan was my guide, and together we feasted on delicacies from India, Malaysia, China, and other Asian countries.

Gado-gado

3 hardboiled eggs, shells removed

200 g green beans, trimmed

3 medium-sized potatoes, peeled and cubed

$1/2$ teaspoon ground turmeric

$1/6$ cabbage, cut into large squares

1 continental cucumber, peeled, seeded and
   sliced into batons

12 pieces puffy tofu (deep-fried beancurd), halved

PEANUT SAUCE

220 g roasted peanuts, crushed

440 ml water

1 stalk lemongrass, finely chopped

4 cloves garlic

2 tablespoons *sambal olek*

1 medium-sized onion, chopped

150 ml vegetable oil

1 tablespoon salt

3 tablespoons sugar

$1/2$ tablespoon paprika

2 tablespoons tamarind water (made as per the
   instructions on page 115)

🍜 SERVES 6 AS AN ENTREE

To prepare the vegetables. Deep-fry the hardboiled eggs quickly in smoking oil until they are golden brown. Cool and cut in half. Blanch the beans quickly in salted boiling water until they are cooked but still crisp. Cook the potato in salted water with the turmeric until tender. Cook the cabbage in salted boiling water.

To make the peanut sauce. Simmer the peanuts in the water until a thick mixture forms. Combine the lemongrass, garlic, *sambal olek* and onion in a food processor. Gently cook the paste in the oil until fragrant and the oil seeps through (about 30 minutes). Add the paste to the peanut mixture with the salt, sugar, paprika and tamarind water and cook for a further 20 minutes.

Toss the cucumber and tofu with the eggs and cooked vegetables, arrange on a dish and pour over the peanut sauce.

Gado-gado was originally an Indonesian dish and has become a very popular Malaysian salad. This is the Nudel Bar's version.

OPPOSITE AND BELOW   The Hawkers' Market is one of the most popular events at the annual Melbourne Food and Wine Festival. Crowds of people come to sample the delicious food and be entertained.

Reef cod cooked in ginger flower broth

This dish from Near East restaurant uses *bungan kantan*, fresh wild ginger flower (*Etlingera elatior*), which is difficult to find and very expensive. Frozen ginger flower is readily available from Asian grocers.

500 g reef cod fillets, sprinkled with salt

1 bud wild ginger flower, finely sliced

3 tablespoons oil

2 cups fish or chicken stock *or* water

$^1/_2$ teaspoon shrimp paste (optional)

2 teaspoons ground dried chilli paste (optional)

3 tablespoons sugar

$^1/_4$ cup lime *or* lemon juice

1 teaspoon salt

6 kaffir lime leaves

4 okra, sliced

REMPAH

4 cloves garlic

2 medium-sized red onions, diced

1 thumb-sized piece ginger, sliced

2 red chillies, sliced

🦐 SERVES 8

To make the rempah. Blend the garlic, onion, ginger and chilli together.

Heat the oil in a saucepan and sauté the rempah for about 10 minutes. Add the stock and chopped ginger flower petals. Add the shrimp and chilli pastes, if using, and then the sugar, lime juice, salt and kaffir lime leaves, checking for taste. Put a small amount of oil in a separate non-stick pan and fry the fish lightly, 1 minute each side, until coloured. Transfer the fish to the broth, add the okra and simmer for a further 2 minutes. Serve.

QUEEN VICTORIA MARKET

The Queen Victoria Market has been operated by the Melbourne City Council for 110 years. As cities all over Europe abandon their central fresh food markets, or work hard to re-establish local growers' markets (as in North America), we in Melbourne have an extraordinary resource available to everyone. It currently occupies 7 hectares. The Queen Vic market, as it is affectionately known to thousands, has remained essentially intact, both in the services it provides and as an historical landmark. Stalls are still paid for by the traders on a daily basis and merchandise is removed from the stalls at the end of each trading day.

There are market families here that have had stalls for generations. Nearly thirty years ago I was a librarian at an inner-city school and among my students were the sons and daughters of Chinese market families. These kids are now the adult stallholders themselves and they call out a friendly greeting when I pass by. Many generations of Melburnians, from all walks of life, have enjoyed and still enjoy the market's unequalled range of high-quality food. The market is conveniently located, the food is sold at reasonable prices and its diversity covers every ethnic group in the wider community. No matter whether you want Halal meat, unbleached tripe, the hottest chillies, organically grown fruit, skinned dried broad beans, fresh okra, live crabs, the freshest green beans or the juiciest strawberries, it is all here!

Years ago there was a lady who used to sell small posies of flowers she had gathered from her own garden. They were wonderfully eccentric – a bit of wild fennel, a few grass flowers, some capeweed, and all sorts of pretty cottage flowers. She used to sit on the corner of another stall where an old man had a basket of second-hand spectacles. People used to try them on and buy them. I guess the community is a bit more affluent now, or maybe the old man died. A ritual which has survived the years is buying a grilled bratwurst sausage dripping with mustard before setting out for the serious shopping.

Having painted this very rosy picture it is worth noting a few warning signs. Convenience rules the lives of many as they work harder and longer hours. Shopping patterns change and grabbing a few things on the way home is tending to replace a more leisurely weekly shop. Like every other resource the market must be used to remain viable. Its support is becoming a little wobbly. And the market management has also changed and with this change has come a shifting of priorities. If support continues to fall, Melburnians may see the Queen Victoria Market shrink dramatically or, too awful to contemplate, sold for commercial development. I hope the Council continues to see the value of the market, not only as the heart of our food-rich city, but as an important tourist resource.

OPPOSITE   Last year I came to the market with a BBC food journalist and he was speechless at the range, the obvious freshness, and above all the relatively low prices, especially of our fish and shellfish. Here we have coral trout (above) and sand crabs, or redspot crabs, as they are known in Queensland (below).

ABOVE   Annual visitors to the Queen Victoria Market number around seven million, making it Melbourne's biggest attraction by far, and placing it well within the top twenty tourist sites in Australia.

OVERLEAF   The market's fabulous range of fruit and vegetables comes from every growing region in Victoria and beyond.

Cameron | *Cameron Russell is a well-known stallholder, although he rented his first stall just five years ago and is a relative newcomer.* Cameron trained as a chef but his love of food is now satisfied by searching out and selling the very best fruit and vegetables he can find. He is also a passionate mushroom enthusiast. In the autumn his stall boasts a collection of mushrooms and, as a sideline, he also organises field trips for other mushroom foragers.

Cameron's stall is labelled 'Stall 83: It is all about flavour!'. If the product happens to be grown on an organic farm that is fine by him, but he is more interested in the flavour and variety than the philosophical beliefs of the grower. In the late summer and early autumn Cameron's stall is a riot of colour from boxes of heirloom tomatoes, including the startling Green Zebra and Black Russian varieties. Very recently Cameron has been granted rights to pick the heirloom varieties of apple and pear that are growing in the small but very old orchard attached to one of Melbourne's historic homes, Rippon Lea. Until Cameron became involved, the fruit on these trees simply fell to the ground. Last year 1000 kilograms of apples were picked. Part of the proceeds from the sale of this fruit goes to Rippon Lea to provide care for the orchard. (Heirloom varieties of fruit and vegetables are those that, for various reasons, are no longer found in general horticulture. Occasionally they are found in old gardens. Their preservation is due to the work of dedicated seed-saver groups around the world.)

One of the most interesting aspects of Cameron's work has been developing a network of suppliers. Many are either home gardeners or have a small orchard of something special, and are delighted to sell direct. This means that at various times one can find on Cameron's stall such interesting crops as sour cherries, blood peaches, Cox's orange pippin apples, golden beetroot and fresh horseradish, items not often found at the wholesale market. Last year I bought some Jersey Royal potatoes at his stall, the first time I had tasted them. They were tiny and waxy and quite outstanding. At this stage the sole grower has decided not to plant them again as the low yield and the lack of familiarity with the variety combined to make them an expensive experiment. Cameron is hoping to interest a group of quality retailers to form some sort of loose network so that specialist growers can be assured of an appreciative market, and food lovers will not be deprived of a special experience. At the time of writing Cameron has a significant wholesale business, which is becoming more and more important.

On this day I was delighted by his display of marvellous pumpkins, all gold and yellow and green, striped, smooth, and warty, and by the shapes and colours of some heirloom eggplant varieties, purple and with a satin sheen, green and striped, and perfectly egg-shaped and white. Nearby was a bucket of thick fresh horseradish roots. Cameron cut me a chunk of musk melon; the fruit was so juicy and its perfume intense. Alongside was a tray of autumn plums, polished to a shine that one would swear was due to wax, but this was not the case.

OPPOSITE AND ABOVE   Cameron Russell's Stall 83 has some of the best-flavoured and most interesting produce in the market, often including little-known varieties and wild mushrooms in season. When we visited it was olive season.

Steamed golden beetroot

1 bunch golden beetroot

extra-virgin olive oil

few drops good-quality vinegar (I like to use
    sherry vinegar)

sea salt

freshly ground black pepper

freshly chopped parsley *or* rocket leaves
    (optional)

Wash beetroot well and steam until tender. Test by piercing with a fine skewer (it should slip in with no resistance). Rub off the skins and halve or slice the vegetable depending on size. While warm, drizzle with oil, add a few drops of vinegar and season with sea salt and freshly cracked black pepper. If you like, sprinkle with chopped parsley or rocket leaves.

If you have lots of beetroot, they can star as a vegetable in their own right. If you have only a few, slice them and arrange them around a platter of tzatziki, or combine them with 'fillets' of fresh oranges, some choice leaves of rocket or baby cos and slices of roasted, peeled capsicum for a first course.

Ian | *Ian Milburn is a farmer from the eastern Wimmera, on the border of the Mallee in north-western Victoria.* His property, Glenloth, was selected by his family in the 1870s. Ian's story is the now-familiar one of a broadacre farmer, in his case a wheat farmer, responding creatively to a fall in prices by diversifying. Ian's first venture was into squab pigeon, those delectable fledgling birds beloved of the French and totally unlike the pigeons we see in our squares and on our public buildings. Ian brought together a group of like-minded farmer friends who agreed to produce and then market the birds collectively. He first came to see me ten years ago to discuss what a restaurateur would require before buying these relatively expensive and luxurious birds. We discussed size, tenderness, methods of plucking and other essential topics, such as delivery schedules, and at the end of our discussion I was convinced we would soon be doing business together. And we did. Since then Ian has supplied most of the best restaurants in Australia with his wonderful squab pigeons, and has followed with pheasants, partridge, silkies (black-skinned bantams) and grain-fed, free-range chickens.

When I spoke to Ian at the market, he said that nothing much had changed in the intervening years. He still mixes the chicken feed most carefully, the birds are still free of antibiotics and they still grow more slowly, still cost more to produce, and still scratch in the dirt. Operations such as Ian's offer no competition to the battery producers, who are selling over 200 000 chickens per week compared with Glenloth's 500–600 birds. But the food lover can make a choice!

Chicken is the all-time favourite in my house for family parties so I had arranged to buy some of Ian's chooks from the Chicken Pantry at Queen Victoria Market, one of his biggest retail outlets in Melbourne. It is not unusual for a Glenloth chicken to weigh in at 2.5 kilograms dressed weight, plenty for eight people. I was thrown into a fever of indecision as to what to do with these beautiful birds. Elena and I considered the options as we strolled through the vegetable section. Finally we decided on the colourful and festive dish of chicken couscous.

OPPOSITE Cameron gave me a bouquet of my favourite golden beetroot, wrapped in tissue like a bunch of roses. These are available in the autumn and seem to 'bleed' less into other ingredients than the usual red variety.

Couscous with grain-fed chicken and vegetables

The word 'couscous' refers to both the round pellets of cooked grain, ground from hard durum wheat, which is served with the meal, and to the meal itself. There are many versions of the meal couscous. They vary from country to country (Tunisian couscous is different from Moroccan and Algerian couscous), and within each the ingredients and flavourings have seemingly infinite variation. The grain expands in the steam that rises from the stew and becomes light and digestible. Almost everyone uses packet couscous, but for the best results steam the grain over a pot of simmering liquid rather than using it just soaked with water as the packet suggests.

A couscoussier is the special two-part utensil designed for cooking the meal. The meat and vegetables simmer in the bottom half, and the top half has a perforated base and holds the grain. If you do not have one of these utensils, the meal can be cooked quite satisfactorily in a deep pot. Try to use a pot over which a metal colander will fit snugly and you can then improvise. Couscoussiers are sold in speciality food stores. To find your nearest supplier you could contact Maison de Tunisie, telephone (03) 9416 1385.

2 x 2.2 kg grain-fed chickens
4 red capsicums, halved, seeded and brushed with
    olive oil
500 g couscous grain
300 ml boiling water
1 tablespoon olive oil
8 medium-sized carrots, peeled and cut into thirds
300 g chick peas, soaked overnight, cooked till just
    tender in plenty of unsalted water and drained
4 medium-sized turnips, peeled and cut into quarters
8 large chunks pumpkin, peeled and rubbed with
    olive oil
harissa to taste (see page 128)
8 medium-sized zucchini, cut into thirds
1/2 bunch coriander, picked over and roughly chopped

BROTH
1 stick cinnamon
3 parsley stalks
3 sprigs coriander
3 litres chicken stock
1 onion, chopped
pinch saffron
3 cloves garlic, chopped
1 teaspoon paprika
1 teaspoon *ras-el-hanout* (see page 128)
4 tablespoons tomato purée *or* chopped ripe tomato
1 hot chilli
sea salt

🐓 SERVES 8 GENEROUSLY

Cut the chickens into 10 pieces each – 2 drumsticks, 2 thighs, 2 wings with part breast and 4 breast portions. (Use the back, neck and giblets to make the stock for the broth.)

To prepare the capsicum. Put the oiled capsicum on a tray and place under a hot grill until the skins are black. Allow the grilled capsicum to steam in a plastic bag until cold and then lift off and discard the blackened skins. Cut the flesh into large pieces.

To prepare the grain. Place the couscous grain in a bowl and tip in the boiling water mixed with the oil. Wait for a few minutes and then fork through. Transfer to a flat tray and with your hands work through all the grain, separating and lifting it to ensure that there are no lumps.

To make the broth. Tie the cinnamon, parsley and coriander with string. Combine the stock, herb bundle, onion, saffron, garlic, paprika, *ras-el-hanout*, tomato purée and chilli in the bottom part of a couscoussier or in a large pot. Bring slowly to the boil, adding salt to taste.

To cook the couscous. Drop the chicken thighs and drumsticks and the carrot into the broth and simmer for 20 minutes. At the end of this time taste the broth. If it is getting very spicy-hot, remove the chilli. (Remember that the heat will be further diluted by extra ingredients so don't be too timid. The dish should be highly flavoured.) Now add the cooked chick peas, turnips, chicken breast pieces and wings, and the peeled capsicum pieces. Simmer for a further 20 minutes. Put the oiled pumpkin chunks into a hot oven to roast.

Remove the bundle of herbs from the broth, and the chilli if not removed earlier. Taste the broth and if extra zing is required, add a little *harissa*. Add the zucchini chunks.

If necessary, rub the couscous again to separate the grains. Transfer to the top half of the couscoussier or to a metal colander that will fit over your pot. Settle it in position over the broth. Cover tightly and simmer for 15–20 minutes. Test the chicken for tenderness and retrieve the roasted pumpkin from the oven.

To serve. I find it best to serve a modest helping of the chicken, vegetables and chick peas in a wide pasta bowl and a portion of the grain in another smaller bowl (a rice bowl is ideal). The broth goes over the chicken, as does a scattering of coriander. This way each diner can see a little of everything and the extra can be kept hot and served in large serving platters when needed. Tiny bowls down the table should hold the *harissa*. Bread should not really be necessary as the grain and chick peas are there for soaking up the juices.

RIGHT Tomatoes and saffron are both used in this recipe. I have used an asparagus peeler to remove the skin of the tomatoes as an alternative to dipping them in boiling water.

Ras-el-hanout

Harissa

Paula Wolfert explains in *Good Food from Morocco* that *ras-el-hanout* literally means 'top of the shop' and that it is a very old mixture of spices, sometimes ten, sometimes nineteen and sometimes more than this. Recipes vary and it is common to find the so-called aphrodisiac flavours of Spanish fly included. It is also common to include dried rosebuds, as well as the less exotic flavours of cumin, ginger, coriander, cayenne pepper, cloves and cinnamon. It is usually very hot and is available in Middle Eastern shops.
I have given Elena's recipe for it, which does not contain any aphrodisiacs and is not too fiery.

BELOW AND OPPOSITE The chicken couscous (see pages 126–7) is an ideal party dish. It is straightforward to cook, looks very festive and is easy to make in large quantities in a couscoussier (below right) or a deep pot.

Dried rosebuds are available in some Middle Eastern stores and also in shops that sell makings for potpourri. I prefer to pick some of my own unsprayed Cecile Brunner rosebuds and dry them overnight in the oven with just the pilot light going, or to hang a bunch in the kitchen for a few days. Once quite dry, keep them in a screw-top jar.

4 whole nutmeg, ground
10 scented rosebuds, dried
3 stalks dried lavender
12 cinnamon sticks
1 teaspoon aniseed
8 teaspoons ground turmeric
1 teaspoon cayenne pepper
2 tablespoons ginger root
6 cloves
1 tablespoon white pepper
8 teaspoons allspice
20 cardamom pods

🕊 MAKES ½ CUP

Grind all the ingredients together in a spice grinder. Store in an airtight container.

After using the food processor for this recipe (and any other involving quantities of chilli), it is a good idea to process a thick slice of bread, together with a tablespoon of sugar, to absorb any scraps of chilli left behind. Rinse all parts of the food processor thoroughly before putting it in the dishwasher, especially checking the interior of the section where the bowl attaches to the motor base.

250 g fresh chillies, seeded and chopped
1 medium-sized head garlic, peeled and chopped
1 tablespoon ground coriander
1 tablespoon ground caraway seed
1 tablespoon dried mint
3 tablespoons fresh coriander leaves
1 tablespoon salt
olive oil

🕊 MAKES 1 CUP

Blend all the ingredients in a food processor using enough oil to make a stiffish paste. Store in a jar, covered with a thin film of oil, for several months. It is very hot!

SYDNEY ROAD

Once I had made the decision to cook a chicken couscous that necessitated chick peas, the couscous itself and the spice mixture *ras-el-hanout*, a trip to Sydney Road, Brunswick, had seemed essential. My first guided tour, a few years ago, was with Melbourne chef Greg Malouf, who is very much at home here and enjoys buying traditional Lebanese goods and using them in a manner often quite different to the way his mother would have done. In this shopping strip, the Turkish, Lebanese and Syrian communities are well looked after by butchers, bakers, delicatessens and pastry-cooks, who sell an intriguing array of specialities, many quite unknown to me. Some I am learning about, such as the sour spice *sumac*, ground from a berry; or *za'atar*, a spice mixture, which is great sprinkled on bread before baking it.

I bought *bastourma* from the Istanbul Halal butcher. *Bastourma* is silverside that has been sugar-cured and then rolled in spices and air-dried. It is sold cut in very thin slices. I was going to use it as the basis for a salad. I bought Turkish bread from Alasya, straight from the glowing woodfired oven. And at the A1 Bakery I watched as baker Elias Farah thrust peel after peel of shaped, seasoned or filled

OPPOSITE AND BELOW   The bright colours and beautiful packaging of Middle Eastern and European products entice buyers in Sydney Road.

bread deep into his oven. He sells more than 1000 of these freshly baked snacks a day. I bought one filled with haloumi cheese that bubbled and melted deliciously. It was so good I went back for another, this time fresh spinach and fetta. Elena had already finished her choice – a round sprinkled liberally with *za'atar*.

At Balha's we selected exquisite baklava, one with a filling of cashews and two with pistachio, and tasted one or two pastries on the spot, including a fat roll filled with clotted cream. I was invited into the back room to watch the fine shreds

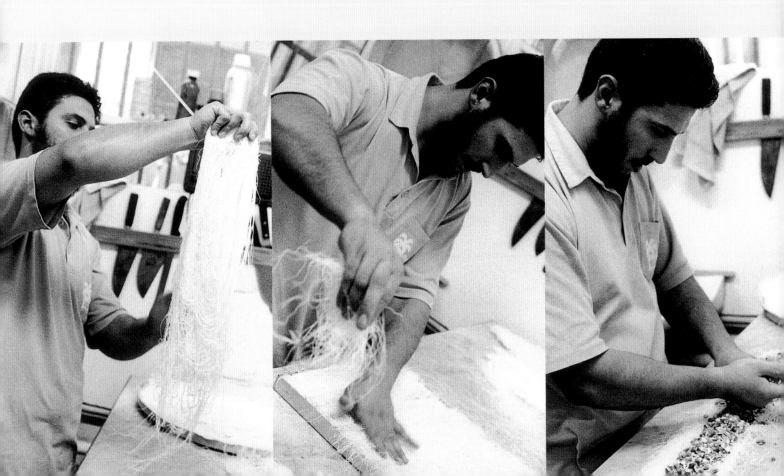

of *kataifi* pastry being extruded like a never-ending thin pencil line directly onto a hot copper plate. The baker scooped the fine strands in his fingers and carefully laid the skein of pastry on a tray before recommencing the process.

As it was early autumn the fruit and vegetable stalls had cases of beautiful pink and green pistachios, along with the first cases of green olives for pickling and the slightly bulbous white zucchini that are so delicious. I couldn't resist any of them.

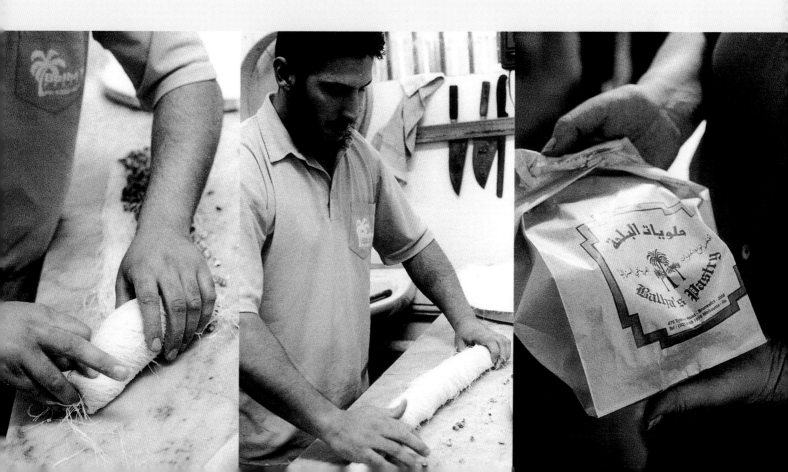

Salad of bastourma, chicken liver and quail-egg croutons

6–12 chicken livers, depending on size

6 slices bread from a Turkish loaf *or* a French stick

2 tablespoons extra-virgin olive oil

2 teaspoons red-wine vinegar

6 quail eggs, cracked and put into individual pots
  (eggcups are a good idea)

18 inner cos leaves, washed and dried

12 thin slices *bastourma* (see page 131)

6–12 labna balls (see below) depending on size

sea salt

freshly ground black pepper

2 tablespoons roughly chopped coriander leaves

1 tablespoon roughly chopped flat-leaf parsley

🕊 SERVES 6

Check the chicken livers carefully and remove any speck of liver that has a greenish stain as this will make the entire liver taste bitter. Brush the bread lightly with olive oil and grill or toast. Keep warm.

Heat a small frying pan with a film of olive oil and sauté the trimmed chicken livers. Allow them to brown well on both sides and then reduce the heat and cook for 1–2 minutes, until they feel springy to the fingertip. Quickly tip in half the red-wine vinegar and toss so that all the livers are flavoured. Remove from the pan and keep warm. Wipe out the pan, add a further film of olive oil and tip in the cracked quail eggs and fry for 2 minutes. Carefully lift out and settle them on the warm toasts.

On warmed plates arrange the cos leaves, *bastourma*, quail-egg croutons and thick slices of chicken liver. Place the labna balls in the cos leaves. Mix the remaining olive oil and red-wine vinegar to a quick dressing, season with salt and pepper and spoon over the crouton and the egg. Mix the coriander and parsley together and scatter over the salad. Serve at once.

Labna balls

Labna balls are delicious on garlic croutons or on opened-out pita bread with salad ingredients. Or serve them with a baked potato instead of butter. They can be scattered with or rolled in finely chopped herbs or ground spices or small amounts of very finely chopped spring onion. They can also be drizzled with honey and a light dusting of cinnamon.

600 ml plain yoghurt

1 teaspoon salt

garlic cloves, unpeeled and bruised

sprigs of rosemary

extra-virgin olive oil

Mix the yoghurt with the salt and drain for 2 days, refrigerated, through a doubled sheet of muslin lining a strainer resting over a large bowl. Roll the mixture into small balls and then store in a flat container. (I find it a good idea not to store them in a narrow glass jar as the balls are quite soft and one risks damaging them while gouging a few out.) Scatter in garlic and rosemary and cover with oil. Leave overnight to allow the flavours to blend. The balls are delicious for at least 2 weeks and I have never managed to have any left longer than this!

OPPOSITE If you are looking for the ingredients for this salad, *bastourma*, labna balls and Turkish bread are obtainable in Middle Eastern shopping strips. Making your own labna balls is simple. At Richmond Hill Cafe & Larder we make and sell labna balls using very rare buffalo yoghurt.

Baba ghanoush

This is Elena's eggplant dip. Tahini is now widely available in supermarkets and will certainly be located in any shop popular with the Middle Eastern community.

3 eggplants
1/2 clove garlic, minced
2 tablespoons tahini
2 tablespoons yoghurt
juice of 2 lemons
2 tablespoons chopped parsley
salt
pepper
cumin and paprika oil (see recipe below)

Roast the eggplants resting on a simmer mat over an open gas flame until charred. Transfer them to a board, split in half and scoop out the soft flesh. Squeeze excess moisture from the eggplant over a basin, holding the vegetable in a piece of muslin or clean tea towel. Combine the eggplant, garlic, tahini, yoghurt, lemon juice and parsley in a food processor. Add salt and pepper to taste and then drizzle with cumin and paprika oil.

Cumin and paprika oil

2 tablespoons cumin seeds
2 tablespoons paprika
2 tablespoons water
2 cups vegetable oil

This oil should be prepared one day in advance. Heat the cumin seeds in a small dry pan over low heat, shaking frequently, until the spice smells fragrant. Grind the cooked seeds to a powder in a spice or coffee grinder, put into a bowl and add the paprika and water. Add the oil, stirring to mix, and then transfer to a clean screw-top jar and shake vigorously. Keep aside for at least one day, shaking once or twice. Strain through a strainer lined with muslin. This oil keeps for several weeks if refrigerated.

Tzatziki

OPPOSITE We served tzatziki on a handpainted majolica platter and decorated it with steamed, peeled golden beetroot and dried mint leaves.

500 g plain yoghurt
100 g light sour cream
1 long cucumber, peeled, seeded and diced
1/2 clove garlic, minced
salt and pepper to taste
1 tablespoon dried or freshly chopped mint

Drain the yoghurt overnight, refrigerated, through a doubled sheet of muslin lining a strainer resting over a large bowl. Tip the drained yoghurt into a bowl and combine with all the ingredients other than the mint. Adjust the seasoning and spread in a flat dish to make it easy for scooping with pieces of flat bread. Garnish with the mint.

RICHMOND HILL CAFE & LARDER

Now two years old, Richmond Hill Cafe & Larder has fitted happily into the neighbourhood of inner-suburban Richmond and into Melbourne cafe life. Seven days a week it offers simple and interesting food, outstanding cheeses and a small but carefully selected range of food products, together with quality books and magazines relating to food and wine.

My partners in Richmond Hill Cafe & Larder are my elder daughter, Lisa Montague, my longtime friend Angela Clemens, and Will Studd. Will is an Officier des Chevaliers du Taste-Fromage de France and a tireless supporter and champion of Australian specialist cheesemaking. In planning my luncheon party I wanted to offer my friends three Victorian cheeses that were in fine condition, while also providing a sampling of specialist sheep's, goat's and cow's milk cheesemaking. Will agreed to assist in the selection and we tasted and chose Meredith Blue, Meredith Caprini and Gippsland Blue, all cheeses that went wonderfully well with a late-picked pinot gris from T'Gallant on Mornington Peninsula. Will recently published his first book, *Chalk and Cheese*, and with his kind permission I have included descriptions of these cheeses as they appear in his text.

ABOVE From the interior of the Richmond Hill Cafe & Larder patrons can look out onto busy Bridge Road, crowded on weekends with people shopping for clothes or homewares, and football fans on their way to the Melbourne Cricket Ground.

OPPOSITE Three excellent examples of Victorian specialist cheesemaking: Gippsland Blue (top), Meredith Blue (right) and Meredith Caprini (front).

MEREDITH BLUE

Producer: Meredith Dairy (Vic)
Classification: farmhouse
Form: 500 g and 1 kg rounds, paper wrap
Milk: ewe
Average fat: 29 per cent
Rennet: calf
Rind: natural
Best season: autumn and late winter
Description: The natural grey dusty rind covers an ivory-coloured interior that is flecked with blue–green mould, depending on season and maturity. The cheese is most popular when soft and satiny with sweet, herbaceous hints of grass and herbs.
Additional notes: This is Australia's first farmhouse blue cheese made from pure ewe's milk and was developed by Richard Thomas and Julie Cameron. While it is quite variable depending on the season, at its best it is a delicious benchmark cheese.

MEREDITH CAPRINI

Producer: Meredith Dairy (Vic)
Classification: farmhouse
Form: 70 g upright tapered cylinder, paper wrap
Milk: goat
Average fat: 25 per cent
Rennet: calf
Type: traditional
Best season: spring and autumn
Description: When young this cheese has a thick, chewy rind and a dense, slightly chalky interior with a pleasant, herbal tang. It matures to a sensuous, soft, flowing texture with a mild, clean and creamy goat aftertaste.
Additional notes: A good example of a goat's milk cheese that is distinctive and interesting but not too aggressive. Ideal enjoyed mature as an individual cheese.

GIPPSLAND BLUE

Producer: Tarago River Cheese Company (Vic)
Classification: farmhouse
Form: 5.5 kg wheel sold in halves or quarters, foil wrap
Milk: cow
Average fat: 26 per cent
Rennet: Halal calf
Rind: natural
Best season: late spring and early winter
Description: The natural grey crusty rind is flecked with orange and white moulds, and the interior ripens to a soft, sticky, creamy texture punctuated with grey and steely-blue veins. Rich in flavour with hints of pasture, and ammonia as it ages. Best when bought from the whole wheel.
Additional notes: Australia's first farmhouse blue cheese was developed by Laurie Jensen, Richard Thomas and farmers Rob and Lyn Johnson. The combination of yeasts and mould cultures used in this cheese has produced one of Australia's finest benchmark specialist blue cheeses.

Passionfruit bavarois

vegetable oil
3 gelatine leaves
cold water
200 ml milk
125 g castor sugar
4 egg yolks, lightly beaten
60 ml strained passionfruit juice
30 ml passionfruit pulp
1 cup cream, softly whipped

🕊 SERVES 8

Lightly brush 8 x 125 ml moulds or a 1.25 litre ring mould with vegetable oil. Soak the gelatine leaves in the water until softened. Warm the milk and sugar in a pan until the sugar has dissolved. Pour the warm milk mixture into the egg yolks, and then return to a moderate heat in the rinsed-out pan. Cook, stirring, until the mixture coats the back of a spoon. Squeeze the softened gelatine leaves and drop into mixture. Stir until dissolved (maybe 1 minute). Strain into the bowl of an electric mixer and beat until cold.

Add the passionfruit juice and pulp and gently fold in the cream. Pour into the prepared moulds and refrigerate until set. Turn out to serve and spoon over a little freshly scooped pulp or place a halved passionfruit alongside.

Alternative method. Strain the custard into a bowl resting over another bowl filled with crushed ice. Stir until the mixture starts to thicken. Then proceed with adding the juice, pulp and cream. The only difference between these methods is that beating the mixture until cold results in a final texture that is a little airier.

BELOW   The texture of a bavarois is best on the day it is made. Remove it from the refrigerator at least half an hour before serving to soften a little.

OPPOSITE AND OVERLEAF   I gathered roses from my garden to decorate the house and provide petals for the table. Elena (menu page, top right) and my daughters, Lisa (centre left) and Holly (bottom right), helped to serve the meal.

THE LUNCH

A relaxed and long lunch in the garden with family and good friends is as close to perfect happiness as I can contemplate. With my profound interest in all things culinary, the pleasure includes the planning, the considering of options, the final decisions, the shopping, the cooking, the setting of the table, the tidying up of the garden, and then the conversations and the flavour of the wine, and the flavours of the food, and the oohs and aahs of the company, the languor and, a long long time later, toast and tea and an early night.

We started with a pretty table, set with bowls of fresh pistachios and pickled turnip for nibbling, and with warm Turkish bread and eggplant dip and a yoghurt and cucumber dip, all accompanied by a glass of the very special Cuvee 2000 from Domaine Chandon in the Yarra Valley. We were anticipating the new millennium with this wine!

Next the salad of thinly sliced *bastourma* with fried quail-egg croutons and some of the delicate little balls of buffalo yoghurt labna from Richmond Hill Cafe & Larder. The salad was sort of like a Middle Eastern Caesar salad, or a rather unusual variation of bacon and eggs. But it looked very colourful and had the right mix of soft and crunchy, salty and soothing, warm and cold. With this course we drank a 1998 Prentice Whitfield Pinot Grigio.

The big production was the chicken couscous. Cooked in my beautiful copper couscoussier it filled the kitchen with aromas of chilli and saffron and cinnamon. Even more so as the lid was lifted from the steaming grain and I started to ladle broth over the portions of chicken and vegetables. Small bowls of *harissa* were placed strategically so that each guest could adjust the heat appropriately. With this couscous I chose one of my favourite wines, Crittenden's 1997 I Sangiovese. It was quite a while before we moved onto the cheese platter as the couscous was so irresistible that guests helped themselves to seconds and in some cases thirds!

The cheeses were accompanied by T'Gallant Late-picked Pinot Gris. With many blue cheeses a late-picked wine of this type is a more satisfying marriage than a red wine. The tannins in the red wine can sometimes make the blue cheese taste metallic. Much, much later lunch finished with a velvety passionfruit bavarois, the baklava – arranged exquisitely on a platter with the palest pink rosebuds – and coffee. And one of my guests, poet Chris Wallace-Crabbe, was persuaded to read his poem in praise of passionfruit.

Passionfruit

used to be plump and glossy
but his mackintosh has shrunk
as he sucks in his cheeks
while somewhere inside the room
he is giving you the pip
with a wonderful sour sweetness
like last year caught in a daydream,
the tang of paradise.

Chris Wallace-Crabbe

LUNCHEON MENU

❦

Fresh pistachios
Pickled turnip
Baba ghanoush
Tzatziki
*Domaine Chandon
Cuvee 2000*

❦

Salad of bastourma,
chicken liver and
quail-egg croutons
with labna balls
*Prentice Whitfield
Pinot Grigio 1998*

❦

Couscous with
grain-fed chicken,
vegetables and
harissa
*Garry Crittenden
I Sangiovese 1997*

❦

Caprini from
Meredith Dairy
Gippsland Blue from
Tarago River Cheese
Company
Meredith Blue from
Meredith Dairy
*T'Gallant Late-picked
Pinot Gris*

❦

Passionfruit bavarois

❦

Baklava from Balhas
with coffee

clear

water

Tasmania's North-East

Clean air, clear water, sharp outlines, brilliant colours, friendly people and not many of them – it has to be Tasmania! Once known as the Apple Isle, Tasmania is now far more diverse in its offerings. It is not surprising that industries that depend on a quality natural environment have been very successful: aquiculture, winemaking and cheesemaking, to name some of them, although Tasmania still grows sensational apples.

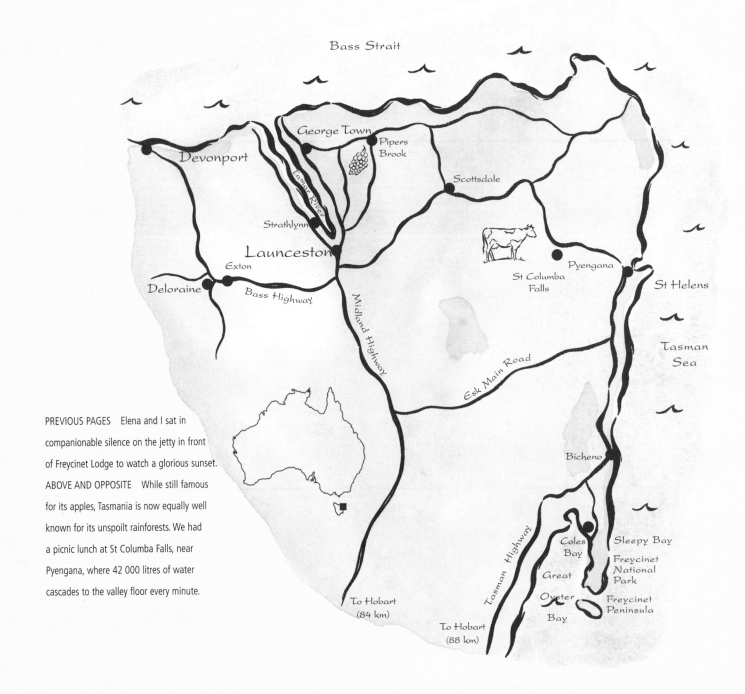

PREVIOUS PAGES   Elena and I sat in companionable silence on the jetty in front of Freycinet Lodge to watch a glorious sunset. ABOVE AND OPPOSITE   While still famous for its apples, Tasmania is now equally well known for its unspoilt rainforests. We had a picnic lunch at St Columba Falls, near Pyengana, where 42 000 litres of water cascades to the valley floor every minute.

Mainlanders sometimes make the mistake of thinking that Tasmania is a small place, especially when judged by its size on the map of Australia. However, Tasmania, our largest island, covers 63 000 square kilometres, of which more than 40 per cent has been set aside as national park. One can spend whole days travelling the excellent roads of the state and see remarkably few travellers (sadly what one does see in abundance are the remains of hundreds of native animals that have wandered trustingly onto the roads).

But the state's small population creates its own pressure. Unemployment remains a serious problem, especially for young people, and it is more difficult for businesses to succeed – expensive freight costs, for instance, are a fact of life for all. The most viable enterprises export to the world as well as the mainland. The success stories are of those that specialise, produce high-quality and desirable products, and offer high-quality services that celebrate Tasmania's natural beauty. Tasmania must and does aim for the top end of the market.

PIPERS BROOK VINEYARD

Sabrina and Andrew | *I first met Sabrina and Andrew Pirie eight years ago when their daughter Isabella was in a stroller and their beautiful vineyard was very new and in its first stage.* I remember the fierce pride with which Andrew described his philosophy of winemaking – it was clear he was only interested in the very best – and I remember just as vividly the superb chewy bread made by Sabrina for our lunch, and the salad leaves she picked from her own tiny garden, newly planted outside the home that she and Andrew lived in on a hill above the winery. The bread was so delicious that I adopted it as the bread to be made each day at Stephanie's Restaurant. (Elena was wide-eyed in wonder – she had done two years of her apprenticeship with me and had never realised that there actually was a Sabrina!)

Andrew planted his first vines in 1973 and ten years later he showed his young bride exactly where the new winery would be. He was a man of his word, with a clear vision of where he wanted to be.

Isabella is now nine years old. The kitchen garden has matured. Close to the house is a small plantation of oak trees that may hopefully yield some truffles in a year or two. Andrew is still uncompromising and every bit as determined to make fine wine. He has just launched his first sparkling wine as part of the winery's twenty-fifth birthday celebrations, and Pipers Brook Vineyard is now listed on the stock exchange. It is among the top eighty wine producers in Australia (and the Pipers Brook group accounts for 35 per cent of the Tasmanian wine industry). The beautiful winery is three times the size it was when I first saw it. The espaliered pear trees on its sunny walls are bearing (the fruit would be a lovely finish to our lunch), and Andrew is convinced that the only way forward for Tasmania is to aim at the highest-quality end of the market in all its endeavours.

We tasted some wines from the barrel and Andrew was ready to play the game of this goes with that. We theoretically ate a globe artichoke with the 1998 riesling, and a Heidi Gruyère and onion tart with the 1998 gewürztraminer.

When I posed the challenge of deciding our luncheon wines to match oysters, followed by grilled eel, followed by cheese and onion tart, Andrew had no problem in suggesting Pirie 1995 with the oysters, followed by 1998 Pipers Brook Riesling to cut the oil in the eel and to balance the richness of the cheese. He spoke of the wine's 'racy acidity'. I found it fascinating to listen to an expert talk through a wine. Andrew's advice, if attempting to place the aromas of a wine, is to take a very deep sniff and then imagine to what part of the kitchen this smell would lead – to the spice cupboard, to sweet jams, to the garden perhaps for green leaves, or maybe to fresh bread or even toast. A different approach!

OPPOSITE AND ABOVE   Andrew and Sabrina Pirie have created a beautiful vineyard and winery at Pipers Brook, which now has a flourishing cafe and cellar-door showroom to better accommodate the large number of visitors.

There is a well-marked Wine Route brochure guiding the visitor to other wineries of the Tamar Valley and Pipers Brook region. Many offer cellar-door sales, and some serve meals. One such place, the Strathlynn Wine Centre, is located on the western side of the Tamar River near the township of Rosevears and provides cellar-door tastings and sales of Pipers Brook Vineyard and Ninth Island wines. It was created by Sabrina Pirie and offers simple yet elegant meals in a delightful setting looking onto the Tamar River and over vineyards that are part of the Pipers Brook holdings.

The original Sabrina bread

OPPOSITE   At the Strathlynn Wine Centre, also owned by the Piries, I enjoyed Sabrina's delicious homemade bread. Sabrina agreed to start a batch for our lunch while we set out to gather the other ingredients.

Sabrina and I discussed the ratio of yeast to flour and I realised that my suspicions had been correct. My own chefs had allowed the amount of yeast to increase in order to hasten the rise. The rule '2 teaspoons of dry yeast to 2 kilograms of unbleached flour' is what the originator of this loaf decrees. 'And the first rise will take overnight.'

1 teaspoon instant dried yeast
2 teaspoons sea salt
500 g unbleached plain flour
300 ml water
a little semolina
poppy *or* sesame seeds

🕊 MAKES 3 BREADSTICKS

Mix the yeast and salt with the flour. Place in an electric mixer with a dough hook and add the water. Knead for 5 minutes, or knead by hand for 10 minutes, until the dough is smooth and feels springy. (Sabrina suggests that the properly kneaded dough should feel like a woman's breast.) Place the dough in a lightly oiled bowl, cover, refrigerate and allow to rise for 8–10 hours.

Once the dough has doubled, ease it onto the workbench. Fold it into four and return it to the bowl for a second rise of 2–3 hours. Once it has doubled again, ease the dough onto the bench. Divide it into three pieces and cover the pieces that are not being shaped. Flatten each piece into a rectangle and roll into a breadstick shape. Place seam-side down on a floured tea towel. Leave to recover, covered, for 45 minutes. Preheat the oven to 220°C.

Sprinkle three baking trays with fine semolina. Gently roll the breadsticks from the cloth onto the baking trays, again seam-side down, and sprinkle with poppy or sesame seeds, or dust with plain flour. Quickly slash the top of the breadsticks with a very sharp knife or razor and place in the preheated oven. Cook for about 25 minutes, spraying the sides of the oven with water after the first few minutes, and then every 10 minutes.

CLEAN WATER AND OYSTERS

On my first morning in Tasmania I poured myself a glass of water as part of my usual wake-up ritual. I was astonished at the quality and the coldness of this elemental beverage. Tasmania is like this – the simple things are so good.

Andrea | *Coles Bay, a tiny town with a population of around 120, is 120 kilometres from Launceston at the entrance to the Freycinet National Park.* It is here that Andrea Cole has her oyster farm. Oysters are filter feeders and depend on their environment to remain healthy and to become plump and succulent. In various locations around this clean, wild coast Tasmanian Pacific oysters have developed an excellent reputation and the industry is worth $15 million a year to the state. Andrea's company, Freycinet Marine Farm, has operated from the same location for eighteen years. Tasmania has colder waters than other oyster-growing regions in the country, with the result that it can provide good-quality oysters for many months of the year. In other parts of Australia the water is warmer, especially in summer – and oysters spawn in warmer waters. When they spawn they lose firmness and become milky, and are not pleasant to eat at this time. If the water temperature of Coles Bay rises too much during December to March, Andrea moves her oysters to a deepwater farm with even colder temperatures in the aptly named Great Oyster Bay, located between the Freycinet Peninsula and the east coast. And it was from this deep water that she had gathered some sea lettuce for me to use in a salad I was planning to make for lunch the next day (see page 174).

Andrea describes herself as 'greener than the greenest' and stresses that she is still getting the same growth rates in her oysters as she did eighteen years ago due to careful farm management. This includes leaving parts of the farm fallow each year to permit recovery. Most of Andrea's customers are supplied direct and appreciate the care and personal attention they are getting. And of course Andrea likes to know that her oysters are going to good homes!

The craft used to load the heavy frames was significantly named *Perseverance*. Each oyster is handled about six times before final harvesting and on average will be two years old. Andrea brought in oysters to be delivered that evening to nearby Freycinet Lodge. She donned waders and walked into the icy sea to retrieve the frame she wanted. The oysters were graded by hand, washed by a steam hose and then delivered, unshucked, to be opened at the moment of ordering for the ultimate pleasure.

Andrea gave us a lesson in safe oyster opening. We were intrigued that she went into the oyster at a midway point along the side of the shell, not the hinge end as both Elena and I were more used to. Andrea downed quite a few herself and said how she missed the flavour of the oysters if she was away from home for more than a day or so. I enjoyed my first samples just seconds from the sea. They were briny and delicious. I demonstrated to Elena how a freshly opened oyster will curl its frilly gills in protest at a squirt of lemon juice, and how this is widely used as the test of a fresh oyster in France. In Australia it is still common to sever the muscle that attaches the oyster to the shell and flip the oyster meat over to present a smooth humped look, rather than leaving it spread in the shell and still firmly attached. A cut oyster is of course a dead oyster! Andrea and I both sighed at the difficulty in convincing the Australian public that it is best to enjoy oysters in autumn and winter as is known and done in Europe, rather than consider them as a summer treat when they are much more likely to be spawning.

We drove over to the national park to watch the sunset and walked out on the wooden jetty in front of Freycinet Lodge. The rocks seemed to be a pink-lavender colour, and the water was deep but so clear that we could watch the gentle movement of the seaweed. There was barely a splash or a ripple and we waited in silence as the last light faded. Perfect peace.

Oysters Rockefeller

M.F.K. Fisher includes a recipe for Oysters Rockefeller in *Consider the Oyster* and concludes her recipe with the remark, 'Oysters à la Rockefeller any place but *chez* Antoine are not quite as delicious, not quite as *kosher* nor as *comme il faut*'. Well, I don't know about that. Apparently Oysters Rockefeller has been on the menu at Antoine's Restaurant in New Orleans since 1899. I have eaten at Antoine's but for some reason did not order this speciality. I have eaten some pretty splendid Oysters Rockefeller cooked under the direction of Gay Bilson on a memorable occasion at the National Gallery in Canberra, venue for the never-to-be-forgotten surrealist banquet for the Seventh Symposium of Australian Gastronomy in 1993. My recipe is very loosely based on that given by M.F.K. Fisher.

3 dozen large Tasmanian Pacific oysters, unopened
rock salt
100 g unsalted butter
3 shallots, finely chopped
2 inner stalks celery, chopped
1 small sprig thyme
1/2 bunch spring onions, finely chopped
1 1/2 cups blanched cooked spinach, chopped
1 tablespoon Pernod
1 tablespoon Worcestershire sauce
1/2 cup oyster liquor
salt and pepper to taste
1/2 cup very fine fresh breadcrumbs

SERVES 6

Open the oysters and immediately tip the juices through a fine sieve resting over a small bowl. Release each oyster from its shell, slipping it into the sieve so that all its liquor may be collected. Rinse and dry the shells. Slip the oysters back into their shells and settle them on a baking tray spread with a layer of rock salt, so that each shell sits firmly.

Melt half the butter and when it is foaming sauté the shallots, celery, thyme and spring onion, stirring, until the vegetables are limp. Stir in the spinach, the Pernod and the Worcestershire sauce. Add the oyster liquor and bring rapidly to the boil until the mixture seems moist but not sloppy. Blend in a food processor with the pulse action until the sauce is smooth and thick. Beat in the rest of the butter.

Taste for seasoning. Spoon the green sauce over each oyster and sprinkle generously with breadcrumbs. Without delay pass the oysters under a hot grill or place them in a very hot oven for just long enough to have the sauce bubbling and the crumbs browned. If there is to be a delay, spoon over the sauce but do not add the crumbs until you are ready to proceed.

A word of warning. The oyster shells will be extremely hot and it is easy to burn one's mouth, so attack these oysters with a fork or spoon rather than attempting to tip the contents into your mouth. Ouch!

Steamed oysters with sea lettuce

For this dish you need bamboo steaming baskets, easily and cheaply available from Chinese supermarkets and Asian grocery stores. To have all the oysters ready at once will require four baskets and two saucepans half-filled with boiling water. Each basket will comfortably hold nine oysters without any 'piggybacking', and each saucepan can support two baskets. Or steam the oysters in two batches, in which instance your guests will have to wait for their seconds.

3 dozen oysters, unopened but well scrubbed
sea lettuce, well washed and broken into
   small pieces
2 tablespoons water
200 g unsalted butter, cut into pieces
juice of 1 lemon
black pepper *or* Tabasco

🦪 SERVES 4–6

Arrange the oysters in the bamboo baskets and scatter over the pieces of sea lettuce. Have saucepans of water already bubbling, waiting to receive their baskets. Guests also should be ready and waiting.

Bring the water to the boil in a small saucepan and whisk in the butter, piece by piece. Don't be too tentative about this. Just lift the pot away from the heat if the butter seems to be getting so hot that the creamy emulsion risks turning to oil. Once all the butter is in and melted and the sauce is lovely and creamy, squirt in the lemon juice, and season with the black pepper or Tabasco. Divide the sauce between the guests, maybe in eggcups or some such container.

Settle the steamer baskets in position, put on the lids and wait for 5 minutes. The shells will have partly opened. Quickly lift each basket onto a dinner plate and carry to each guest, who now lifts an oyster, spoons on a little butter sauce, nibbles a piece of sea lettuce and moves onto the next oyster. Provide teaspoons for the sauce, an oyster opener in case someone needs to help an oyster to open a little wider, and big napkins.

OPPOSITE   We stole a peaceful moment during our hectic shooting schedule to look at beautiful Sleepy Bay, across the peninsula from Coles Bay.

BELOW   Thick gloves are needed for handling oyster trays in very cold water. A proper oyster knife, as well as gloves, should be used when opening the sharp-shelled molluscs.

CHEESEMAKING AT PYENGANA

We drove for over an hour on steep and winding roads to arrive at Pyengana. In the front gardens of the few wooden houses we passed were laden fruit trees: apple, quince and pear. Some houses offered tomatoes or greengage plums for sale. At Pyengana, in the far north-east of the state, cheese is made in the same way it was in 1895 when Terence Healey, the present owner's grandfather, was farm manager in what was then a dairy-farming cooperative.

Jon and Lyndall | *Today Jon Healey and his wife, Lyndall, own Healeys' Pyengana, a company formed in 1992, and they milk more than 120 Friesian cows.* There is one important difference between the original cheese and the one made today: nowadays all the milk is required to be pasteurised. But Pyengana cheddar is still cloth-wrapped in the traditional way and left to mature on wooden boards in the impressive maturing room. The cloth wrap reinforces the cheese and acts as a natural breathing rind. I spoke to Jon, who was enjoying morning tea with Lyndall and their rosy-cheeked one-year-old daughter, Isabella. Jon was born here and has no interest in living anywhere but in this beautiful valley of the George River, with its chocolate-brown rich soil and thickly wooded hills. Today the grass was sunlit but Jon assured me that he can count on an annual 47 inches (1194 millimetres) of rain.

Cheese is made most days and, for those with very discerning palates, apparently the finest flavours are present in cheeses made from spring and autumn milk. Cheesemaking is a satisfyingly straightforward process. At Pyengana the cows are brought in from the fields to be milked twice a day, the milk is pumped into the cheesemaking vat, starters are added and the milk is heated. The resultant curds are broken up by hand and scooped into hoops and left to drain. The cheeses are taken from the hoops, pressed overnight and then imprinted with the date of manufacture, cloth-wrapped and transferred to the maturing room. Here they are turned and wiped every day for the first six weeks, and then every three days until they are ready for sale, a minimum of six months later. Jon is passionate in explaining the importance of milk quality. He runs fewer cows on his farm than it could sustain in order to maximise their condition.

Much of the equipment is shining and new but Jon is very proud of the nineteenth-century (Victorian) bedpress still used to press the larger cheeses, and the old 40-pound hoops used in his grandfather's day and which he purchased from the defunct Pyengana Cooperative factory. Another relic of times gone by is the old milking shed that was used continuously for more than fifty years.

In the maturing room were rows and rows of yellow cheeses. When fully loaded the room holds 7 tonnes of cheese. Jon makes cheeses in various sizes ranging from the smallest at 1.5 kilograms to the largest 18-kilogram rounds. Each size has a name, for example, the smallest cheeses are 'truckles' and the 5-kilogram

ABOVE AND OPPOSITE Jon and Lyndall Healey's dairy farm at Pyengana is in the George River valley, an Arcadian landscape of sunlit emerald-green valleys dotted with black and white Friesian cows, outlined against a hazy blue backdrop of folded hills of gum and blackwood.

cheeses are 'top hats'. Lovers of Pyengana cheddar prefer their cheese to be aged. Jon will not sell his big cheeses before they are six months old and for good customers he will look after their cheeses for a further six months. The smallest cheeses mature faster. Some cheese wholesalers and retailers mature the cheeses further; for example, at the Richmond Hill Cafe & Larder we take pride in offering Pyengana cheese that is at least eighteen months old. I noticed several cheeses with names and notes attached, such as 'Mr Trebilcock will collect cheese at Christmas time'.

The Healeys are enterprising marketers and a resourceful family. Excess milk is strikingly packaged and labelled as Real Milk and is sold through approximately fifty outlets in northern Tasmania. For the last seven years the Healeys have also sold cheese through their farm shop, along with Real Milk milkshakes! Last summer 4 tonnes of cheese was sold through the farm shop, about 40 per cent of total production (more than 90 per cent of it to visitors from the mainland, many of whom are on their way to visit the nearby St Columba Falls). Visitors can also purchase a Ploughperson's Platter. The shop sells pickles and preserves made by Jon's mother, including pickled eggs and pickled onions; miniature fruit cakes made by his mother-in-law; and biscuits made by one of his sisters.

Alas, the recipe for the fruit cakes sold at Pyengana is a closely guarded secret. I went to Elizabeth David's *English Bread and Yeast Cookery* and found a small section devoted to spiced fruit breads. David in her inimitable scholarly way gives numerous bibliographic references to support her contention that 'the custom of eating cheese with these spiced fruit breads or cakes, is a very good one. The cheese should preferably be a Wensleydale, a Cheshire or a well-matured Lancashire'. I tried her recipe for North Riding Bread, omitting the almond essence and slightly increasing the milk (see page 161), and found it pretty good with Pyengana matured cheddar.

Mushrooms on toast

This is a superb recipe for gathered mushrooms. If you are not able to pick your own, the recipe still makes cultivated mushrooms taste wonderful. Always use fully opened 'flat' mushrooms to cook this way. These mushrooms are delicious atop a grilled steak, too.

16 mushrooms, each about 10 cm in diameter
1 clove garlic, cut into thin slices
2 tablespoons butter
freshly ground pepper
water
freshly chopped parsley
hot toast, well buttered

🍲 SERVES 4

Trim the stems of the mushrooms. Discard any sandy or dirty trimmings and chop the rest of the stems finely. Place mushrooms, garlic and chopped stems in a wide pan with the butter and grind over the pepper. Add 1 cm of water to the bottom of the pan and cover tightly with a lid. Cook over moderate heat for 10–15 minutes. Lift the lid. The mushrooms should look black and smell heavenly.

To reduce the juices, turn up the heat and remove the lid. Boil fast, shaking gently to prevent sticking and turning the mushrooms once or twice in the juices. Those who are extravagant may add an extra nut of butter at this stage! Scatter parsley over the top and pile onto hot, crunchy well-buttered toast.

Cheddar popovers

For this recipe you will need a muffin pan that makes 12 muffins. I have also made tiny popovers that cook in 10 minutes using ovenproof eggcups, but small brioche tins would be ideal, too.

2 x 55 g eggs
pinch salt
$^1/_2$ teaspoon paprika
finely grated zest of $^1/_2$ lemon
1 tablespoon parsley, freshly chopped
2 shakes Tabasco
3 tablespoons plain flour
125 ml milk
2 tablespoons olive oil
75 g Pyengana cheddar, coarsely grated

🍲 MAKES 12 POPOVERS

Break the eggs into a bowl, add the salt, paprika, lemon zest, parsley and Tabasco, and whisk well. Sieve in the flour and whisk until smooth. Gradually stir in the milk and leave the batter to stand for 20 minutes. Preheat the oven to 220°C.

Divide the olive oil between the muffin holes and place the muffin pan in the hot oven for 5 minutes to get really hot. Carefully take it out and pour in the batter to half-fill each hole. Divide the cheese between the holes and quickly replace the tray in the oven and set the timer for 20 minutes. The popovers should be well risen, crisp and brown. Eat at once!

ABOVE   While searching for a 'beauty shot' we came across a hillside strewn with field mushrooms. We picked about twenty and then wondered how to enjoy them given that we were staying in very basic motel units. The solution was to send the cheekiest member of the team to the kitchen of the local pub to ask the chef to cook them for us. He was happy to oblige. So dinner was grilled scotch fillet and a big bowl of our mushrooms simply cooked with butter, a touch of salt and some freshly ground pepper. They were magnificent.

OPPOSITE   Pyengana cheese is wrapped in a double thickness of muslin and stamped with the date of manufacture.

Spiced fruit bread

450 g plain flour

$^{1}/_{2}$ teaspoon salt

4 teaspoons baking powder

120 g lard *or* butter

170 g brown sugar

170 g seeded raisins

170 g currants

85 g mixed peel

1 tablespoon treacle

300 ml milk

🍞 MAKES 3 LOAVES

Preheat the oven to 190°C. Butter three 13 cm x 7 cm deep round tins and line with paper. Sift the flour with the salt and baking powder. Rub in the lard or butter and sugar. Mix in the raisins, currants and mixed peel. Stir in the treacle and milk to mix to a soft dough. Spoon into the tins and bake for about 50 minutes, until the fruit bread tests clean when pierced with a skewer. Allow to cool completely and then wrap in foil to keep for at least a week.

Pickled onions

1 kg small onions, peeled

3 tablespoons cooking salt

1 litre good-quality wine vinegar (traditionalists would insist on malt vinegar)

2 teaspoons allspice

2 teaspoons whole black peppercorns

1 cinnamon stick

Place the onions in a glass or ceramic dish and sprinkle with the salt. Leave overnight. Next day rinse and pack the onions firmly into clean dry jars. Boil the vinegar with the spices.

For very crisp pickles, allow the vinegar mix to cool completely before filling the jars. Cover with a disc of kitchen paper and then seal the jars. Wait at least two weeks before using.

For a softer pickled onion, pour the pickling vinegar over the onions straight from the stove (a little at a time in each jar first of all to prevent cracking). These onions will be ready to eat in a week.

OPPOSITE   Apples and pears can be found for sale at roadside stalls in many parts of Tasmania. These beauties sit in a bowl made by the renowned Tasmanian potter John Campbell.

BELOW   At St Columba Falls Elena and I enjoyed our picnic lunch of Pyengana cheese, fruit cake, pickled onions and apples. The attractive stoneware mugs decorated with a happy cow were made by Lee Farrell, one of Jon Healey's sisters.

POPPY SEEDS, ONIONS AND TRUFFLES

We drove west through open bushland and admired the seemingly endless landscape of sunlit gum trees with red-and-gold new tips and peeling trunks. I wanted to see opium poppies growing. Poppies have always been one of my favourite flowers and for twenty-one years diners at Stephanie's Restaurant ate from plates edged with a raised art nouveau design of poppies, including a lavender one! I had assumed this colour was a flight of fancy until I saw a poster of a field of beautiful pale lavender poppies growing in Tasmania. They were opium poppies and I soon found out that the location of the fields is shrouded in secrecy. Tasmania's relative isolation is seen as an advantage in the poppy-growing industry as it enables close supervision of such a sensitive crop. More than 600 farmers grow these poppies throughout the state.

After flowering the petals drop and the plants are left to dry naturally. The seed pods (or capsules) are then harvested mechanically and processed to retrieve morphine for the pharmaceutical industry. A by-product of the harvest is the poppy seed that many of us enjoy on our bagels or dinner rolls or in luscious cakes and strudels. Our main competitors in growing poppy seed for culinary purposes are Turkey and Eastern Europe. I was surprised to learn that poppy seed contains 40 per cent oil, which is no doubt why poppy-seed cakes are so filling.

BELOW AND OPPOSITE   Driving along a back road, we came upon this paddock of brown onions, harvested and drying, shining golden in the sun.

We followed instructions and arrived at the designated field to find it bare – the harvest had taken place a week earlier! Never mind, I had been given a bag of Tasmanian poppy seeds and I could still try out my recipe for poppy-seed strudel.

And just across the road was a paddock shining with golden orbs. They were harvested brown onions, laid out to dry in the sunshine, and they did look beautiful. A young lad who was probably the farmer's son drove up on his four-wheeled motorbike as we hung over the fence admiring the colours against the red soil.

'Haven't you ever seen onions before?' he said scathingly. Well, I think the truth was that we had never seen so many, in such beautiful shining rows. He roared away, shaking his head, his hair as blond and tawny as the onion skins, I thought!

Just days before this book went to press, the first magnificently perfumed black truffles (*Tuber melanosporum*) were harvested in the northern part of the state near Deloraine. This elusive and mysterious fungus is one of the most prized ingredients in classical French cookery. After seven long years of waiting, Duncan Garvey and Peter Cooper, principals of Perigord Truffles of Tasmania, and the successful grower, Tim Terry of Tasmanian Truffle Enterprises, have proved the doubters wrong and are looking forward to an exciting future. All food lovers congratulate them and salute another example of Tasmanian enterprise.

Poppy-seed strudel

1 egg white

castor sugar

icing sugar

SWEET YEAST DOUGH

2 teaspoons instant dried yeast

$^1/_2$ teaspoon salt

250 g unbleached plain flour

150 ml milk

25 g sugar

50 g butter

POPPY-SEED FILLING

150 ml milk

100 g poppy seeds

50 g ground almonds

25 g butter

2 tablespoons honey

3 tablespoons homemade fruit mincemeat

grated zest of 1 lemon

2 egg yolks

SERVES 10

To make the dough. Mix the yeast and salt with the flour in the bowl of an electric mixer fitted with a dough hook. Warm the milk with the sugar and drop in the butter. Stir until the sugar is dissolved and the butter is just melted. Cool for a minute and then beat the liquid into the flour until you have a smooth dough. Cover the bowl and let the dough double (about 1 hour).

To make the filling. Bring the milk to the boil and pour it over the poppy seeds. Return the milk and seeds to the heat and stir until the mixture simmers. Cook for 5 minutes, stirring all the time. Remove from the heat and add the remaining ingredients. Allow to cool completely before using.

To assemble and bake. Once the dough has doubled, preheat the oven to 180°C and butter a 35 cm square baking sheet. Roll the dough on a well-floured work surface until you have a square that will just overhang the dimensions of the baking sheet and is 5 mm thick. Transfer the rolled-out dough to the baking sheet. Spread the filling to within 3 cm of each edge. Roll up like a Swiss roll and seal each end with a fold of dough and a firm pinch. Flip the roll onto its seam and gently ease it into a horseshoe shape. Allow to rise, covered, for 30 minutes.

Brush the roll with a little egg white and scatter with castor sugar. Bake for 40 minutes. Cool the strudel on a rack and dust with icing sugar. This strudel is best if eaten one or two days after baking.

OPPOSITE   This poppy-seed strudel is made with a tender yeast crust. I like to serve it with plenty of whipped cream.

HEIDI FARM CHEESE

Frank | *Frank Marchand learnt his craft in his native Switzerland and came to Australia in 1974 to work with one of Australia's best-known cheesemaking firms, Lactos.* In 1985 he set up his own small specialist cheese factory, Heidi Farm Cheese, at Exton. Considered one of Australia's finest cheesemakers, he concentrates on making cheeses that he understands well and his Matured Gruyère was voted Champion Cheese at the Specialist Cheesemakers Show in Melbourne in 1998, one of a great number of awards and accolades he has collected.

Frank has had to adapt and modify traditional Swiss cheesemaking to suit Australian conditions. And not only by using pasteurised milk. In Switzerland it is usual for each farmer to own just a few cows and milk them for only a short few months. The milk is pooled and the big cheeses are made cooperatively and are deliberately designed to mature slowly and to last through the severe winters before the cycle recommences. In contrast, here in Exton, Frank can purchase suitable milk from a local farmer through spring, summer and autumn and can even make some cheese in winter.

The most famous of his cheeses is without doubt the Heidi Gruyère, closely followed by his emmental and raclette. I got up very early one morning to observe the process. Frank's assistant, a young man newly arrived from Switzerland, told us that nowadays in his home country much of the actual cheesemaking has been mechanised and is controlled by computers without the need of human expertise. Not here in Heidi!

The vat of creamy junket is cut with a fine wire cheese knife and worked to very small fragments. It is then cooked and when judged ready is pumped into moulds. (The whey is drained off and fed to the cows.) I watched in fascination as Frank flipped newly formed cheeses, dripping with whey, each weighing nearly 50 kilograms, into the press. No wonder he has massive arm and shoulder muscles! After pressing, each cheese is lifted in and out of a brining tank before being laid to rest in the maturing room. One batch yields six mighty gruyère wheels, each weighing around 35 kilograms after pressing. Each cheese is rubbed with brine, hand-turned and nurtured for a minimum of six months until it is considered sweet and nutty and with the characteristic elastic texture of the style. Some of the cheeses exhibit tiny internal holes or bubbles and are poetically described as 'cheese with tears'. The maturing room smells powerfully of ammonia as the cheese matures.

Frank has just successfully negotiated to sell his business to Lactos and is to be retained as specialist master cheesemaker, giving him what he most craves – unlimited time to devote to cheesemaking while leaving others to deal with the business aspects. He seemed pleased with the prospect of new challenges and more time to concentrate on and refine his craft.

OPPOSITE   A traditional fondue is ideal for a cold winter's night but one must have a heavy earthenware fondue pot, a table burner capable of keeping the mixture hot, long-handled forks to permit the safe dipping of the bread into the pot, and a hearty appetite.

Cheese fondue

Any version of fondue is very rich. It is a good idea to serve small bowls of pickled vegetables and maybe thin slices of air-dried ham to nibble on while the cheeses are melting, and a leafy salad to counteract the cheese. Select a sturdy bread for the dipping – cottonwool bread from the supermarket will just crumble away from the fork and be lost forever in the bubbling pot.

1 clove garlic
200 ml dry white wine
250 g gruyère, coarsely grated
250 g emmental, coarsely grated
1 teaspoon potato flour *or* cornflour

60 ml kirsch
freshly ground black pepper
10 slices sourdough *or* other substantial bread,
   cut into large cubes (allow 8 cubes per person)

🍴 SERVES 4–6

Peel the garlic and rub the chosen pot well with it. Throw the clove into the pot or discard it depending on your whim. Pour in the wine and once it starts steaming and before it is simmering drop in the cheeses. Stir continuously using a wooden spoon. Mix the flour with the kirsch and tip into the pot. Continue to stir. Grind in pepper to taste. Start dipping!

There are variations between Swiss and Savoyard fondue recipes, mainly in the types of cheese used, which include emmental, beaufort, raclette and comte. This recipe uses Frank Marchand's gruyère and emmental. In terms of wine, a pinot gris or riesling from Pipers Brook would make this a very special fondue.

Gruyère and onion tart

A variation to this recipe is to replace half the gruyère cheese cubes with some cubes of pumpkin. Roll the pumpkin cubes in olive oil and bake in a hot oven until tender and then cook and rest exactly as above. Both tarts are ideal accompanied by a leafy salad.

BELOW AND OPPOSITE We served our gruyère and onion tart quite simply, with Sabrina's bread and a large green salad.

DAMIEN'S SHORTCRUST PASTRY

180 g unsalted butter

240 g plain flour

pinch salt

3 tablespoons water

TART FILLING

1 large onion, finely diced

2 teaspoons olive oil

750 g gruyère, cut into 1 cm dice

6 eggs

3 egg yolks

3 cups cream

white pepper

sea salt

3 tablespoons freshly chopped parsley

SERVES 8–10

To make the pastry. Remove the butter from the refrigerator 30 minutes before making the pastry. Sieve the flour and salt onto a marble pastry slab or workbench. Chop the butter into smallish pieces and toss lightly in the flour. Lightly rub to combine partly. Make a well in the centre and pour in the water. Using a pastry scraper (and being mindful of the technique you have observed of mixing cement) work the paste to a very rough heap of buttery lumps of dough. Using the heel of your hand, quickly smear the pastry away from you across the workbench. It will combine lightly. Gather together, then press quickly into a flat cake and dust with a little flour. Wrap the pastry in plastic film and refrigerate for 20–30 minutes.

To line the tin and bake blind. Roll out the pastry, dusting generously with flour as necessary. Wrap it around the rolling pin and let it unroll over a 32 cm x 4 cm deep fluted tart tin. Press it firmly into the edges of the tin and trim the edge. (It is usual to roll the pin over the top of the tin to give a very clean edge. With very short pastry, such as this one, I prefer to cut the edge with a knife 1 cm higher than the edge of the tin and fold it over, as it is inclined to shrink during baking, even after chilling.) Chill or freeze the pastry case for at least 20 minutes before baking. Preheat the oven to 200°C.

Line the pastry with foil and fill this with dried beans or chick peas, or some pastry weights that you keep for this purpose. Bake for 15 minutes, and then remove the foil and weights and bake for another 5 minutes. Pour the warm filling into the pastry case while the pastry is still hot. This prevents any liquid seeping through the pastry.

To make the tart filling. Sauté the onion in the olive oil until it is quite soft but not coloured. Tip into a bowl with the diced cheese. In another bowl lightly whisk the eggs and yolks. Warm the cream to scalding point and pour over the eggs, whisking to mix but not to make frothy. Strain into a jug and adjust seasoning.

Place the blind-baked tart shell on a baking sheet for extra stability and put it on the pulled-out oven rack. (It is easy to spill liquid from a just-filled tart shell, so it makes sense to have the tart shell already in the oven.) Scatter in the onion–cheese mixture. Gently pour the egg custard over the back of a large spoon to minimise the disturbance to the onion and cheese. Scatter the tart with the parsley and slide into the oven. Lower the oven temperature to 180°C and bake until the tart is just set (about 20 minutes). Allow the tart to settle for at least 10 minutes before cutting.

Open fruit tart

BELOW   An open fruit tart such as this is the ideal way to use fruit in season. The juices from the hot fruit ooze into the yeast dough, so the tart is best eaten hot or warm.

The yeast dough used in the poppy-seed strudel recipe on page 165 is delightfully easy and ideal for an open fruit tart. For the filling, you can use apples, plums, nectarines, blackberries, pears or gooseberries, or a mixture of fruits.

1 quantity sweet yeast dough (see page 165)
prepared fruit
1 egg, beaten
castor sugar
cream for serving

🦅 SERVES 10

Preheat the oven to 225°C. Roll out the dough to a thickness of about 7 mm and place it on a baking tray that has upturned edges to catch any drips. Allow the dough to puff a little (30 minutes). Gently prick the surface with a fork and cram on a tight layer of fruit. Brush the edges of the tart with beaten egg. Strew the fruit generously with the sugar and place in the oven. After 10 minutes reduce the oven temperature to 180°C. Bake for 25–35 minutes, depending on the fruit chosen. The edges may look very dark and high-baked but this is as it should be. Serve with farm cream.

TASMANIAN EELS

Ranicar family | *Eels Australis is situated in Deloraine, 50 kilometres west of Launceston, and the Tasmanian arm of the company is operated by the Ranicar family.* Wild eels are caught, processed (some are smoked, some are simply gutted) and packed and almost all are exported to Germany. John Ranicar says that there is not much local demand for these creatures, as opposed to the market in Germany, where eels sell for twice the price of smoked salmon. I had enjoyed grilled eel in Japan and was very keen to try and replicate the dish. The eels we were supplied with were about 1 kilogram each but John said they can grow up to 2 kilograms. The larger fish are best smoked. The salad was my own invention, encouraged by the bucket of very fresh bright green sea lettuce given to me by Andrea Cole.

My own memories of eel are of my grandfather catching them in the local creek, beheading them and bringing them home for Mum to skin. She had no experience of eel and had read that one poured boiling water over them. I must have been about ten years of age and can clearly remember my horror as she poured the hot water over the eels in the sink and they all flipped themselves onto the kitchen floor and squirmed about. And then there was the time I took delivery of a parcel of dead eels from the fishmonger, two hours after they had been killed, and realised with horror that the whole parcel was pulsating!

My instructions, therefore, were that the eels should be freshly killed, gutted, and still! Our luncheon guests looked on fascinated as Elena loosened the skin around the head of each eel, rubbed salt on her hands to get a better grip and ripped off the skin in one fast action. The dish was a great success.

Susie's smoked eel pâté

500 g skinned and boned smoked eel, chopped

75 g unsalted butter

125 g mascarpone *or* soft goat's cheese

salt and pepper to taste

dash of Tabasco

juice of ½ lemon

fresh herbs (optional)

In a food processor, pulse the eel for a couple of seconds to break it down. Add the butter and cheese and combine until smooth. Add the salt and pepper, Tabasco and lemon juice and adjust the seasoning as necessary. Transfer the pâté to a small dish and refrigerate. If making to serve the same day, add some fresh herbs.

This recipe for eel pâté, kindly supplied by Susie Ranicar, is particularly delicious with very dark rye bread.

Marinated grilled eel

3 fresh eels, gutted (not smoked)

MARINADE
$^1/_2$ cup mirin
$^1/_2$ cup light soy sauce
2 tablespoons brown sugar

🐟 SERVES 6–8 AS AN ENTREE

To make the marinade. Mix the ingredients together and set aside.

Loosen the skin around the neck of each eel but do not cut off the head. Dip your right hand into coarse salt to get a good grip as eels are notoriously slippery. Pull hard until the skin starts to come away and then rip it off in one action. Cut the eel into pieces about 6 cm long. Using a small knife, fillet each section. Drop the filleted pieces into the marinade and leave for at least 10 minutes.

Lightly oil the bars of a hinged grill and place the eel fillets in it. Place the hinged grill on a Hibachi or charcoal grill. After 3 minutes, turn and open the grill and rebrush the eel with the marinade. The marinade should look glossy and rich in colour. After a further 3–5 minutes in the grill, the eel is ready to serve. Place the pieces on a platter on top of a sea lettuce salad (see page 174), steamed rice or hot noodles.

BELOW AND OPPOSITE   To cook this dish you will need a hinged grill or a fine-grid cake rack that you are prepared to sacrifice (the eel pieces need to be supported on something and the bars of most barbecues are too far apart), and a Hibachi or similar charcoal-burning grill, with hot coals. The grilled eel is here presented on a salad of crisp-cooked beans, cucumber, sea lettuce and Asian flavourings

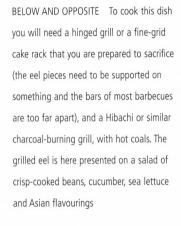

Sea lettuce and ginger salad

2 cups green beans, cooked till just a tiny bit crunchy,
quickly refreshed in ice-cold water and instantly
drained on a clean cloth

3 long cucumbers, peeled, seeded and cut into
thin strips

1 cup sea lettuce, torn into small pieces
and tough bits discarded

bean-thread vermicelli, soaked in boiling water
for 5 minutes and drained well (optional)

2 teaspoons vegetable oil

1 tablespoon toasted sesame seeds

1 tablespoon pickled ginger, sliced into julienne strips

DRESSING
¼ cup light soy sauce
¼ cup rice vinegar
1 teaspoon sesame oil
1 tablespoon lemon juice
½ teaspoon finely chopped hot chilli
1 teaspoon grated ginger

SERVES 6–8

To make the dressing. Mix all the ingredients
together and taste for balance. (Any extra
dressing will keep well for a week in a screw-
top jar in the refrigerator.)

To make the salad. Prepare the vegetables.
Cut the cooked beans into 5 cm pieces. If you
are using the bean-thread vermicelli, cut the
soaked noodles into 5 cm pieces as well. Heat
the vegetable oil in a non-stick frying pan and
quickly sauté the sea lettuce, in small batches.
Each batch will take only a moment to become
bright green and shiny. Tip the sautéed sea
lettuce into a large bowl and toss with the
cucumber and green beans. Add enough
dressing to make the salad moist but not sloppy.
Toss the salad and spread it down the centre of
a long platter. Scatter with the toasted sesame
seeds and the pickled ginger.

WILD BLACKBERRIES

The area around Deloraine is very pretty. It is an historic township, settled in the early 1820s with many original buildings in use as shops, galleries, teahouses and overnight accommodation. We took an inadvertent detour (a bit of poor navigation on my part) but it took us into narrow country lanes, for all the world like the English countryside with high hawthorn hedges, the pretty berries hanging in rose-red clusters, mingled with blackberries that had escaped the spray. The blackberries were ripe for the picking, and pick them we did. I spurred on my companions with the promise of Grandma's famous bramble pie, for which I needed a good quantity of fruit!

Grandma's bramble pie

2–3 cups blackberries

1 egg, lightly mixed with a pinch of salt

1/3 cup granulated sugar

60 g unsalted butter at room temperature, cut into
  small pieces

LARD PASTRY

100 g plain flour

100 g self-raising flour

pinch salt

100 g lard

90 ml cold water

🕊 SERVES 6

To make the pastry. Sift the flours together with the salt. Rub the lard in quickly. Make a well in the centre and work in the cold water. Knead until you have a fairly soft, springy and elastic dough (2–3 minutes). Form into a flat disc and chill for 20 minutes. Preheat the oven to 200°C.

To assemble the pie. Roll two-thirds of the pastry into a circle approximately 26 cm in diameter. Transfer this circle onto a slightly larger buttered oven-proof plate. The pie must be assembled on the serving plate, as it is impossible to move. Roll the remaining pastry into a circle 12 cm in diameter and 6 mm thick.

Tip the fruit onto the larger circle to form a heap. Pleat the sides of the pastry around the fruit so that it starts to resemble a mob-cap, with the pleated edges leaning slightly inwards to the pile of fruit. Rest the smaller circle lightly on top. The lid should sit like a flat plate and extend just beyond the edge of the pleats. Do not seal the lid or press it down heavily, as it has to be removed after baking.

To cook. As some juice may run during the baking, put a metal tray with an upturned edge underneath the pie plate. Brush the pastry with the egg and bake for 25 minutes until the pastry is cooked and golden brown.

To finish. Take the pie from the oven. Using a flexible spatula, carefully lift the lid and tip in first the sugar and then the butter. Replace the lid and leave the pie in a warm place for at least 5 minutes before cutting and serving in wedges. The butter will have melted most deliciously. (Be prepared. Use a spoon as well as a knife and lifter for serving. There will be plenty of delicious juice, which will flow into the pie plate as you cut.) Serve with the very best cream.

OPPOSITE   Sea lettuce is lettuce-green and almost translucent, and floats in small clumps. Its 'leaves' are wavy and about 4 cm wide. It looks tender and edible and it is. As with all shellfish and seafood one must be sure that the water is clean. There was no doubt about that with this sea lettuce, which was gathered by Andrea Cole at Freycinet. Another wild and lovely part of the east coast is Bicheno (below).

ABOVE   There is a compelling fascination in pulling one more prickly branch forward to claim the juiciest and sweetest blackberry, even though one's hands are stained purple and arms and face are already scratched.

THE LUNCH

Our lunch table was set between rows of twenty-five-year-old riesling grapevines, sheltered from any wind. These vines had produced the fruit we were about to enjoy in the 1998 riesling. Our guests assembled and Sabrina carried out the platter of oysters. Andrew opened and poured the sparkling wine and we all sniffed it appreciatively and sipped most enthusiastically. I proposed a toast to Pirie 1995, and thanked Sabrina and Andrew for their generosity. There is a great tradition of offering hospitality to pickers and vineyard workers at vintage time, usually accompanied by local dishes and the opportunity to taste the new wine. This luncheon could be seen as part of that tradition, even though vintage at Pipers Brook was still two or three weeks away.

BELOW   We ate lunch in the vineyard at Pipers Brook among vines bursting with fruit.
OPPOSITE, CLOCKWISE FROM BOTTOM LEFT Grilled eel and sea lettuce salad; Pyengana cheddar and pears; Sabrina Pirie; Andrea's oysters; Stephanie tasting some cheese; Andrew Pirie at the head of our table.

LUNCHEON MENU

❦

Andrea's oysters from
Freycinet Peninsula,
freshly shucked and
on the half shell

❦

Grilled wild eel
on a sea lettuce and
ginger salad

❦

Heidi Gruyère and
onion tart with
a green salad

❦

The original
Sabrina bread

❦

Pyengana cheddar and
pears

❦

Wines
Pirie 1995
Pipers Brook
Riesling 1998

harbour

picnic

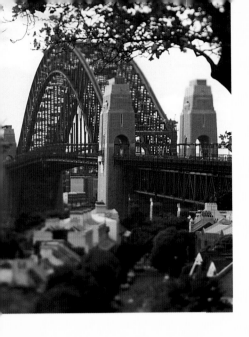

Sydney

I know Sydney as a holiday city. It can be glittering and glamorous, exciting and frenetic, beautiful and steamy, but above all it is fun. Sydneysiders are relaxed in their approach to eating and the city has many places where one can sit and admire the harbour and enjoy the seafood for which the city is justly famous. Often it will be fish and chips served in a no-fuss manner, sometimes something a bit more challenging.

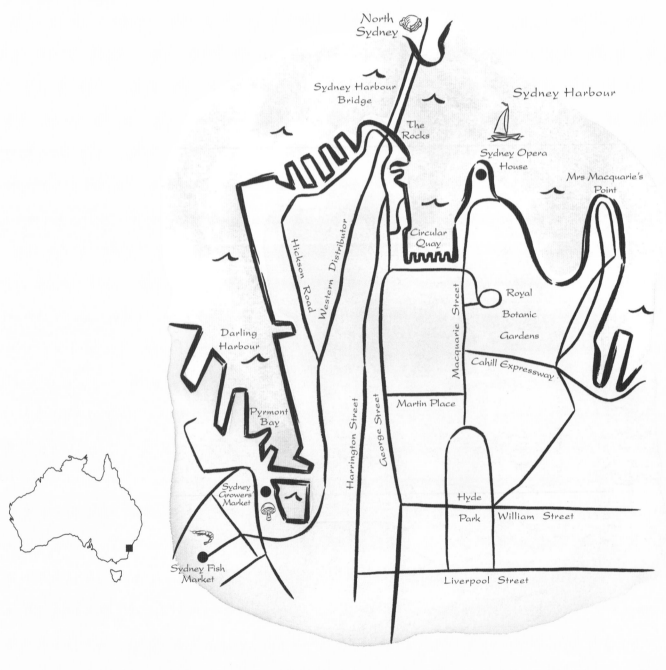

As Sydney gears up for the 2000 Olympics, the city can be downright uncomfortable. Footpaths are being uprooted, roadworks are ubiquitous, buildings are being renovated, scaffolding is everywhere. But the mood is very positive, with most Sydneysiders looking forward to their three weeks in the international spotlight. Business appears to be booming.

Commentators in Sydney and Melbourne waste an awful lot of energy drawing comparisons between each city. The two places are as different as New York is from San Francisco, or London from Bristol. And is it not difference that gives life much of its savour?

Sydney has a delightful climate, especially in autumn and spring. In summer the temperatures soar but so does the humidity and the city steams and goes a bit mouldy here and there. One can walk the 6 kilometres from The Rocks to Mrs Macquarie's Chair, breathing in the briny tang of the water and feeling virtuous for being part of the early-morning traffic of joggers, walkers and cyclists. The harbour is a heady sight as the first ferries chug out churning the water to a snowy froth, the cruise boats rock at anchor and the opaline sails of the Opera House light up with the morning sun. Further out are dozens of small craft, leading to speculation that surely every Sydneysider must own a boat!

PREVIOUS PAGES AND OPPOSITE
Most people visiting Sydney seek out the incomparable Opera House and the Harbour Bridge.
BELOW   A popular spot is Mrs Macquarie's Chair, so named because the governor's wife is reputed to have sat here and gazed out at the great harbour.

Many mornings after completing this walk I have lingered in the Royal Botanic Gardens to enjoy the splendidly laid out herb garden. There are dozens of interesting specimens, with labels that describe uses. I was interested to read that the fruit of the citrus chinotto is best candied when bright green. I have one of these very decorative plants in my own garden and have always been disappointed in the orange fruit. The herb garden has a tasting bed and the public is invited to pick a leaf and have a nibble. A mouthful of holy basil with its spicy aftertaste is sure to wake up the tastebuds!

I have several good friends who live in Sydney so I have spent many a happy hour enjoying the city's fine restaurants. One can eat very well here at every price level and even at the top the prices remain reasonable by world standards. Sydney has its share of the nation's top chefs and consistently high marks are achieved by such as Tetsuya Wakuda, Neil Perry, Tony Bilson, Tim Pak Poy, Damien Pignolet and many more. Janni Kyritsis has a special place in this story as he and I met when we were both more or less learning the trade and we often share a laugh about the old days and acknowledge that we have come a long way since then.

Janni | *Janni was introduced to me in 1976 by a young man who helped occasionally in the kitchens of the first Stephanie's Restaurant.* 'I have a friend who is very interested in cooking – do you think he could come and help once or twice a week?' This was to be the beginning of a significant friendship.

I well remember the first task I asked Janni to help with. It was to bone some quail. In retrospect it seems quite extraordinary that I should expect that someone with apparently little or no experience in the kitchen should be able to do such a delicate thing. Maybe he had already shown his dexterity? Maybe he volunteered? I cannot remember. What I do remember is the way he approached the task. The tiny birds were dealt with exquisitely. A neat bowl of bones appeared and the fleshy

BELOW   One can spend a tranquil, fragrant and instructive hour in the herb garden at Sydney's Royal Botanic Gardens. It is roughly divided between Asian and European herbs of both culinary and medicinal interest. All the plants are well labelled and there are inviting seats tucked against warm stone walls.

OPPOSITE   Elena and I had great fun being with Janni in his own kitchen and we learnt a lot, too.

bodies were laid perfectly one on top of the other. The board was wiped spotless and then he took the bowl of prepared stuffing and with a knife divided it into twelve equal parts and proceeded to stuff and sew the quails with speed and unbelievable finesse. I was speechless.

Throughout the five years we worked and talked alongside each other every day, Janni revealed a highly creative mind capable of leaps of lateral thinking, so that unusual solutions were proposed that worked. He did not ever waste a second and his energy and commitment to the task at hand were inspiring. As a former electrician, he was also able to install or repair thermostats and deal with much of the everyday machine breakdown that seems to be part and parcel of kitchen life.

I envy his young staff at the MG Garage restaurant. There would be few places in the world where one could learn so much – not in the classical sense of mastering conventional technique, but in respect for ingredients and flavour, how not to waste anything at all, how to be cheerful and enjoy working hard, and most importantly, how to make leaps in a culinary sense into unknown territory. Janni's charm is irresistible, his generosity of spirit unparalleled. He shrugs off the slings and arrows that go with the job and can be impatient with whingers and miserly individuals. His private life is sacred and his loyalty to and love for his partner come before all else.

When Janni had suggested preparing a Greek-inspired Easter picnic we both agreed that the perfect location would be somewhere on an island in the middle of the harbour, with beautiful Sydney as a wraparound backdrop. Shark Island was selected – its rocky outcrops reminded Janni of the approach to Rhodes. He had chosen the menu down to the smallest detail. Dolmades and olives to start and then a wild weed pie (*hortapitta*) made with homemade filo pastry, slow-baked legs of lamb flavoured with garlic and preserved lemons and encased in paper, a Greek salad and, to finish, a traditional Greek Easter bread studded with red eggs.

Pickled vine leaves

50 vine leaves (choose young ones)

1 litre water

100 g salt

few sprigs thyme

1 lemon, sliced

olive oil

Place the leaves in a basin and cover with boiling water. Leave for 2 minutes and drain.

Make a brine by combining the 1 litre of water with the salt and bringing to the boil. Allow to cool. Add the blanched leaves to the brine and leave for 2–3 days.

Drain and put into a jar with the thyme and lemon slices and cover with olive oil, pressing down well. Refrigerate for a week before using. These leaves will last for at least 3 months if refrigerated after opening.

ABOVE   We all helped to roll the dolmades, using vine leaves that Janni had pickled in the early summer.

OPPOSITE   Janni's method of preserving lemons is a faster method than I am used to, but the finished product is just as delicious.

Dolmades

24 vine leaves, fresh or canned

$\frac{1}{2}$ onion, finely chopped

150 ml fruity extra-virgin olive oil

$\frac{1}{2}$ cup long-grained rice

$1\frac{1}{4}$ cups water

$\frac{1}{4}$ cup currants

$\frac{1}{4}$ cup toasted pinenuts

$\frac{1}{4}$ cup chopped parsley

1 tablespoon chopped dill

salt and pepper

$1\frac{1}{4}$ cups tomato juice

🕊 MAKES 24

If the vine leaves are fresh, rinse them briefly and cut off the stems. If using canned vine leaves, rinse them well to remove the brine. If using home-pickled leaves (see page 183), there is no need to rinse them. Pat dry and spread on a clean surface.

Sauté the onion in the oil, add the rice and stir well for 2 minutes. Add the water and all the remaining ingredients except the tomato juice. Simmer very gently, stirring from time to time until the rice is cooked (approximately 10–15 minutes). Taste for salt and pepper.

Allow the filling to cool and then divide it between the leaves. Roll up each leaf tightly, tucking the ends in well. Pack the rolls tightly into a saucepan that will hold the rolls exactly in one layer. Pour over the tomato juice. Put a plate on top of the rolls and weight it lightly to hold the rolls firm while they cook. Bring to the boil and then simmer gently for approximately 45 minutes until the leaves are tender. When cool, remove the dolmades to a non-metal dish and store, covered, in the refrigerator. Serve at room temperature.

Preserved lemons

I have become quite addicted to my own Moroccan-style preserved lemons. In my home, grilled fish is quite unthinkable without a few slivers. Janni had a different method to show us. Not for the first time I enjoyed hearing that while methods may vary from culture to culture, a similar condiment is appreciated in a similar way in countries distant from each other.

2 lemons

2 tablespoons salt

1 bay leaf, cut into four pieces

few sprigs thyme

1 cup extra-virgin olive oil (approximately)

Place the lemons in a pot or a basin and cover with boiling water. Leave overnight.

Next day, drain and cover the lemons with cold water. Leave for 2 days, changing the water four times a day. Slice the lemons in 5 mm slices, sprinkle with the salt and refrigerate for a day. Put the sliced lemon in a jar, layered with the bay leaf pieces and thyme sprigs. Cover with olive oil, pressing well, and leave for a week before using.

THE SYDNEY FISH MARKET

This market is perhaps the single most important gastronomic resource for the city. It is run profitably by the Sydney Fish Market Company, set up in 1994, and comprises both New South Wales fishers and onsite retailers. The facts and figures are impressive and there are plenty of them. Suffice to say that on average the market sells 70 000 kilograms of seafood every day, more than 80 per cent of which comes from New South Wales, and more than 90 per cent of those sales are conducted through a silent Dutch auction system. The market's promotional material states that more than 100 species are offered for sale at any given time, which in terms of variety makes it second only to Japan's Tsukiji Market. And more than 1.8 million shoppers visited the fish market during 1997–98 to look and buy from the more than nineteen retailers, ranging from those selling fresh fish to sushi bars and seafood restaurants.

The retail section at the market operates seven days a week from 7 a.m. and the wholesale auction is held every weekday from 5.30 a.m., although the buyers arrive much earlier to inspect the catch. Buyers sit in a tiered stand and the fish is displayed in large open tubs on the floor of the market. There is always plenty of activity, plenty of water and ice and trolleys to watch out for. By 10 a.m. the fishermen and fish merchants are replaced by tourists, shoppers and those looking for a seafood lunch.

BELOW AND OPPOSITE   These swimmer crabs (left), garfish (centre) and plate-sized snapper (right) were on sale at one of several retail outlets attached to the Sydney Fish Market just minutes after they were purchased at the morning's auction.

The market has a very active public relations and marketing department, which must claim some of the credit for the increase in consumption of seafood by Australians from 6.4 kilograms per person in the late 1970s to more than 10 kilograms per person in the mid-1990s. The market also operates a very popular cooking school with its own full-time demonstrators, as well as a year-round program of visiting chefs and foodies who are willing to share their fishy secrets. An interesting fact is that more than 50 per cent of class attendees are male! The marketing department can organise group tours so that interested tourists or locals can see what a vibrant, energetic, colourful place the fish market is at a time when most of us are still tucked up in bed. And it is a sure bet that visitors will see varieties of fish they have never seen before.

James and Costa | *James Demetriou and Costa Nemitsas are passionate about fish.* They confess to even dreaming about it. Given that they start their working day at around 4 a.m. I am rather surprised they have time to dream about anything. They have known each other since school days and seem to have no regrets about abandoning earlier plans to become a schoolteacher (James) and an accountant (Costa). They buy much of their fish at the market but their network extends beyond this and they have direct connections with fishermen all over the country.

Not only do James and Costa take pride in the range of fish they are able to source, but they have pioneered handling techniques that ensure that their deliveries arrive in as near perfect condition as possible. Their packing room is temperature-controlled, handlers all wear gloves to minimise bruising and the fish is handled gently at all times. Fillets are laid out straight in the box and are separated from the packing ice, which can break down the structure of the flesh. It is not surprising that James and Costa's business, Demcos, supplies many of Sydney's most discriminating restaurants.

Janni, Costa and James seem to have a very lively relationship and there was much animated chatter before we were introduced, mostly concerning the day's order for the MG Garage restaurant. Both young men were exceedingly charming and had gone to great pains to provide the 'fishy surprise' that Janni wanted for our picnic lunch the next day. I asked them about Sydney's famous harbour prawns which are so sweet. When in season they are cooked at the market and one can buy a bag and eat them immediately. They were not in season but blue-tailed king prawns were. I had a strong memory of a salad that Damien Pignolet had once made for me that had entailed peeling large quantities of harbour prawns. As they are so small, this is true devotion!

OPPOSITE   This delicious salad successfully combines the briny sweetness of prawns, the suave richness of avocado and the crispness of belly bacon.

ABOVE   My friend Damien Pignolet, owner and chef of Bistro Moncur, was a welcome guest at our picnic.

Damien's prawn salad with a green vinaigrette

200 g belly bacon, skinned and cut into 8 mm batons

180 g curly endive, washed and dried

1 kg small prawns, cooked, shelled and
    digestive tract removed

1 large avocado, cut in half lengthwise, stone and
    skin removed

VINAIGRETTE

½ bunch chives

2 tablespoons French tarragon

2 tablespoons chervil

1 heaped teaspoon Dijon mustard

½ small clove garlic, peeled and crushed to a paste
    with some salt

120 ml extra-virgin olive oil

freshly ground black pepper

30–50 ml tarragon vinegar

extra salt to taste

🦐 SERVES 6

To make the vinaigrette. Assemble everything except the vinegar and extra salt in a blender and purée. Add vinegar and salt to taste and transfer to a container.

Fry the bacon gently in its own fat until coloured and a bit crispy. Drain in a sieve and keep warm. Moisten the endive with some vinaigrette, toss gently and distribute between the plates. Toss the prawns with a little vinaigrette and distribute along with the bacon. Finish with slices cut across the avocado half and a touch more vinaigrette.

The 'fishy surprise' organised by Janni turned out to be giant sea urchins. Janni had a novel way of opening these fish. He first cut out the mouth with a knife and then inserted a strong pair of pliers and forced the handles apart and in so doing split open the urchin shell. The ochre–orange roe was a brilliant contrast to the other black, inedible parts. We scooped the roe and Elena decided that it was definitely an acquired taste. In fact she tried it with her eyes closed and said that she was telling herself it was really caramel ice-cream! The experience is a bit like being hit in the mouth by a strong wave, but for those who enjoy it, the salt tang is balanced by a rich creaminess.

Last year I ate a sublime entrée at Le Pre Catelan, a restaurant in Paris's Bois de Boulogne, where the chef had made a delicate custard of sea urchin and baked it in the cleaned and de-spiked shell until it was just set. Then a layer of celery cream (I think) was spooned over and three 'tongues' of orange sea urchin roe were draped on top. It was an extraordinary dish, rich yet delicate, salty and creamy, warm and cold. I am going to try and replicate it!

Sea urchin custard

One sea urchin contains five 'tongues' of roe so you will need four large sea urchins for this recipe. At Le Pre Catelan the dish was served in sea urchin shells. This entails snipping off all the spines from the shells and cutting a neat top from each one, which is not at all easy to do. I have found it satisfactory instead to serve the delicate custard in small porcelain dishes, such as one might use to bake eggs.

4 large sea urchins
2 tablespoons chervil leaves, plucked from stems
1 shallot, very finely chopped
600 ml cream
3 eggs
2 egg yolks
salt and white pepper
1 tablespoon finely chopped chives

🕊 MAKES 6 DELICATE SERVES

Cut open the sea urchins and tip out the contents. The sea water and black dots are not needed. Carefully extract the tongues of roe (you will have 20 tongues) still attached to the shells and leave on a folded damp clean napkin, covered with plastic wrap, until needed. Discard the shells.

Place the chervil, shallot and cream in a pan with 14 of the sea urchin roe tongues. Warm very gently to simmering point. Turn off the heat and infuse for 1 hour. Rewarm to simmering point and then blend the hot cream mixture until very smooth. Strain through a piece of muslin, pressing well. Whisk the eggs and yolks together, pour in the sea urchin cream and whisk lightly to combine. Taste for salt and pepper.

Lightly butter six small porcelain dishes and pour in the custard. Settle the custard cups in a bain-marie and bake at 160°C for about 15 minutes or until set. Remove the cups from the oven and allow to settle for a few minutes, then garnish with the six remaining sea urchin roe tongues and a scattering of chives.

The Fish Market auction over for the morning, the tubs of fish started to disappear surprisingly fast as suburban retailers wheeled away their purchases. The retail section of the market swung into action as the morning's catch was set out on the display slabs. I admired fish from all over the country – huge black flathead from the New South Wales coast, giant wild barramundi from the north alongside plate-sized farmed barramundi, garfish from Victoria, pretty goldband snapper from the north-west shelf of Western Australia, live mud crabs and brilliant red emperor from Queensland, small cuttlefish and giant octopus, skate wings and sleek tuna and majestic trunks of swordfish, all from local waters. An amazing sight.

We moved on to the sushi bar for breakfast. What dexterity and what a showman! The sushi chef sliced the freshest fish – tuna, kingfish and mackerel – with a razor-sharp knife and carefully moulded each little shape before offering it with a slight bow. The sushi using *uni* (sea urchin roe) was a delight, either wrapped in cucumber or in nori seaweed. Even Elena managed one of these, although she was still unimpressed. I felt that eating the unadorned roe of an entire sea urchin was a bit akin to eating two tablespoons of Vegemite straight from the jar. The intensity of the latter experience would be overwhelming, and not for the faint-hearted, but spread lightly on hot buttered toast it is a morning essential for many Australians. And to eat one or two tongues of sea urchin roe on a plump pillow of vinegared rice, sharpened with a little wasabi and wrapped in crunchy cucumber, was to dilute the flavour and, to my palate, offered a perfect balance of flavour and texture.

OPPOSITE   Giant sea urchins are spiky, frightening-looking creatures that few Australians dare to try. They remind me of the bad Banksia men created by May Gibbs in the Australian children's classic *Snugglepot and Cuddlepie*.

BELOW   It is pretty frenetic at the Sydney Fish Market early in the morning. One needs to keep a sharp lookout for trolleys, ice, slippery floors and men in a hurry.

THE SALAD FARM

Junne and Ray | *June and Ray Henman of The Salad Farm in North Sydney supply many of the city's best restaurants with salad vegetables and cut herbs.* As so often seems to happen with passionate suppliers, they have found their way to their present niche by roundabout means. The growing of plants and herbs started as a hobby but now occupies June full-time; Ray helps with deliveries when he is not making documentary films. The plants are grown hydroponically. Janni in his usual irrepressible way has charmed June and she now grows nettles and purslane for him – and anything else he asks for, it seems. He uses the purslane with pig's trotters, and the stinging nettles and dandelions in his wild weed pie.

Janni spoke of the Greek village tradition where such a pie would include whatever wild greens had been gathered from hillsides and roadsides, as well as one's garden patch. Stinging nettles grew abundantly and were always included, and usually plenty of spinach too. The pie is encased in filo pastry, and of course that too would always have been homemade. A perfect dish to take to a picnic. As Janni rolled, oiled and stretched the nine layers of dough in his kitchen we looked on in admiration. The final flourish was to settle the top crust in position but to let it collapse into loose crumples as it settled. These undulations would rise and become extra crisp, he explained.

BELOW   The brilliant green of the plants Elena, Janni and I saw at The Salad Farm spoke of their exceptional quality and freshness. As far as we could see stretched green and purple salad leaves, variously crinkly, floppy, pointed and rounded.

OPPOSITE   Dandelion (above right and below left), escarole (above left) and red and green oakleaf lettuce (below right) are three of the crops grown at The Salad Farm. Each plant grows in its own individual pot.

Janni's wild weed pie

Janni used spinach, stinging nettles, dandelions, sorrel and chicory for his pie. If using dried oregano, only buy the Greek oregano that is sold on the stem in long cellophane bags.

FILLING

1 kg gathered mixed greens (wild and bitter)

2 medium-sized Spanish onions, finely chopped

150 ml olive oil

salt and pepper

fresh *or* dry oregano to taste

1 egg

500 g ricotta

FILO PASTRY

500 g plain flour

225 ml warm water

1 egg

1 teaspoon salt

1 cup olive oil (approximately)

🌾 SERVES 10

To make the filling. Wash the greens and cook quickly, one variety at a time, in the water still clinging to the leaves, stirring to ensure they cook evenly. Drain very well and chop finely. Cook the onion in the olive oil until quite soft and add it to the chopped greens. Stir in the salt and pepper, oregano and egg. Lightly fold in the ricotta, check the seasoning and set aside until the pastry is ready.

To make the pastry. Mix the first four ingredients together. Knead for a few minutes until the dough becomes smooth and elastic. Rest for 1 hour. Preheat the oven to 200°C.

Cut the dough in half and roll out the first half to a 60 cm square. With a dinner plate as a guide, cut a round in the centre of the square of dough. Leave the round in place and mark the rest of the square into eight roughly equal sections. Brush all with olive oil.

Place the sections, one on top of the other, on the central round. Dust the pile of dough with plenty of flour to absorb excess oil and roll it into a 40 cm circle. Place this circle of dough on a 26 cm pizza tray. Spread the filling right to the edge of the tray and then fold the excess overhanging dough back over the filling to form a pleated edge.

Repeat the rolling, cutting and layering procedure with the reserved half of the dough to form a lid and place it on top, this time allowing the excess to settle into crumpled folds. Brush generously with olive oil. Cook for 20–30 minutes until golden.

SYDNEY GROWERS' MARKET

As Sydney does not have the resource of a centrally located retail fruit and vegetable market such as we have in Melbourne, it is easy to see why people loved the idea of a Growers' Market when it was proposed a couple of years ago. Ten thousand people came to the first Sydney Growers' Market held late in 1998. It brought together home gardeners, orchardists, market gardeners, herb growers, free-range egg producers, bakers and many, many more. Markets such as these are proliferating in foodie communities in North America and I have read that Alice Waters, owner of the visionary restaurant and cafe Chez Panisse in Berkeley, California, found several of her core suppliers at the Ferry Plaza Farmers' Market in San Francisco. I imagine that this Sydney market will go from strength to strength as its popularity increases.

To be an authentic growers' market, all the produce for sale must have been produced by the stallholder. In this way a growers' market differs dramatically from other fresh food markets. There are no intermediaries, or enormous quantities, or tired goods. The market reflects the character of a particular community. The stallholder presents the produce with pride and knowledge, and freshness is beyond question. A visit to such a market is bound to bring a smile to your face and a bounce to your step, neither of which is usual when trailing through a supermarket.

On this market day it poured with rain. But this did not seem to deter the more than forty stallholders who set up at the edge of the harbour at Pyrmont, nor the thousands of Sydneysiders eager to buy from and chat with the growers. In fact the sea of umbrellas and assorted rain gear added considerable colour to the grey morning. I bought a jar of Fig Mostarda, recommended as an accompaniment to

BELOW   At the Sydney Growers' Market one can buy produce direct from the grower. Among the most popular offerings on the day we visited were freshly picked pine forest mushrooms, cultivated Swiss Browns and bunches of cherry-red rhubarb.
OPPOSITE   I learnt that the ground-up shell of an emu egg (left) is reputed to be an aphrodisiac! Janni's butcher, Vic Puharich, specialises in the careful ageing of meat and in this grain-fed lamb (right), a relatively new product.

blue cheese, and a basket of large, shiny Pink Lady apples, discussed a new variety of chick peas and admired the dried fava beans, a relatively new crop being grown in Moree and Walgett in northern New South Wales. We noticed a stall selling scorzonera, and Janni bought a large box of pine forest mushrooms and some slippery jacks from the mushroom forager. Elena and I commented that it seemed that one in three shoppers had a bunch of cherry-red rhubarb poking from their string bag. Rhubarb seemed to have made a convincing comeback.

QUALITY GRAIN-FED MEAT

Vic and Anthony | *Janni next took me to meet his butcher, Vic Puharich, and Vic's son Anthony, of Vic's Premium Quality Meats at Mascot, to collect the lamb for the picnic.* The legs each weighed around 3 kilograms, and were from grain-fed lamb produced at Junee (in southern New South Wales) under the Texel brand. Vic was very enthusiastic about the flavour and tenderness of this meat and agreed that grain-fed lamb definitely cost more.

Alongside Vic and Anthony's passion for grain-fed meat (a relatively new industry in Australia) went an understanding of a very old technique, that of dry-ageing of beef on the bone. Vic appreciates well-aged beef and showed us a hindquarter of beef that had been hanging for nine weeks. Its fat was dry and crumbly and the external colour dark and crusty, but he assured us that within would be cuts of incomparable tenderness. Not surprisingly, to hold, store and age meats in this manner is a very expensive process and accessible only to the most expensive restaurants. The Puharichs also age fillets of beef for up to twelve weeks in vacuum bags for many of their customers.

OPPOSITE When the baking-paper parcel was opened, the slow-cooked lamb with preserved lemon was revealed in all its magnificence. And the aroma was irresistible.

Vic and Janni share a liking for offal. Vic comes from Croatia, where offal is a delicacy. He has been able to supply discerning customers with baby veal kidneys, sweetbreads and beautiful calf's liver that usually leave Australia for more appreciative markets prepared to pay far higher prices than Australians for offal. Vic showed us the pluck, which is the lungs, heart and liver of a lamb that is essential for the Greek dish *kokkoretsi*, often eaten at Easter. Janni described the spitted lamb roast still common in Greek villages. The offal would be cut into small pieces, threaded on one long skewer and held in place by the intestines wound around the skewer. This skewer would be placed in front of the roasting animal and would of course cook much faster and be eaten as an appetiser.

Janni's leg of lamb wrapped in paper

Janni reminded me that in Greece a lamb dish such as this would always be very well done, as would all meat and poultry dishes. The animals scratched out a pretty spare existence in the stony ground and were never as tender as our chickens or our prime spring lamb.

1 x 3 kg full leg of lamb
6 cloves garlic
salt and pepper
10 sprigs fresh oregano *or* 2 teaspoons
    dried oregano
20 slices preserved lemon
¼ cup extra-virgin olive oil

✈ SERVES 8

Preheat the oven to 150°C. Trim the lamb of all extra fat. Peel the garlic, cut each clove into three pieces and roll the pieces in some salt and pepper. Make incisions all over the lamb and insert the garlic deeply into the meat.

Place two 40 cm square sheets of baking paper in a baking tin and oil them lightly. Place the leg of lamb on top. Scatter with oregano and lay the lemon slices carefully all over the meat. Gently drizzle with olive oil. Cover with another sheet of baking paper.

Bring up the paper to form a parcel and fold the edges to seal tightly so that the juices cannot escape. Use a fourth piece of paper to cover the joins. Truss with kitchen string and bake for 2½ hours. Allow to cool in the parcel if serving cold.

Greek country salad

Anyone who has holidayed in Greece will be familiar with this salad of chunked tomatoes, cucumber, fetta cheese and black olives. With richly flavoured olive oil and slightly acidic tomatoes being the preferred choice, the salad stands up well to being carried to a picnic and eaten an hour or so later. Vine-ripened tomatoes that have not been allowed to fully colour are often the preference of Greeks making this salad.

8 tomatoes, cut into chunks

4 Lebanese cucumbers, peeled and cut into chunks

8 spring onions, chopped

2 green capsicums, seeded and diced

extra-virgin olive oil

few drops red-wine vinegar

24 Kalamata olives

freshly ground black pepper

sea salt

fetta cheese, cut into bite-sized chunks
   (allow 3–4 chunks per person)

SERVES 8

Put the tomato into a wide salad bowl and add the cucumber, spring onion and capsicum. Pour over a good slurp of oil and allow to stand for 30 minutes. Add the vinegar and olives. Season, being careful with the salt as some fetta cheese varieties are more salty than others, and mix well. Scatter the fetta over the salad and serve.

Stella's semolina halva

1 cup coarse semolina

½ cup clarified butter

3 tablespoons currants

4 tablespoons toasted pinenuts

2 tablespoons pistachios

¼ cup candied orange peel

SYRUP

1 cup sugar

2 cups water

1 teaspoon ground cardamom

zest and juice of ½ lemon

zest and juice of 1 orange

2 cinnamon sticks

1–2 teaspoons rosewater (depending on strength)

🕊 SERVES 8

To make the syrup. Place the sugar in a pan with the water, stir until it has dissolved and then add all the other ingredients. Strain and keep hot.

Brown the semolina in the butter, add the strained syrup slowly and keep on stirring for 10 minutes until the mixture comes away from the sides of the pan. Add the currants, pinenuts, pistachios and candied peel. Spoon into a lightly buttered 2-cup brioche mould or pudding basin and unmould while hot onto a plate. Serve with lightly whipped unsweetened cream and poached fruit. The pudding is also delicious served cold.

Stella Cheirdari, a young Greek woman whom Janni has taken under his wing and into the brigade at the MG Garage restaurant, had a surprise for us at lunch. She proudly displayed her moulded semolina halva studded with candied peel, almonds and pistachios and drenched in a wondrously perfumed syrup of rosewater, cinnamon and cardamom.

OPPOSITE   It wouldn't be a Greek party without a Greek salad – and of course the olives would be the Kalamata variety, now grown and processed in South Australia.
LEFT   This surprisingly easy pudding was a huge success. The cinnamon, rosewater and cardamom in the syrup evoked the Arabian Nights, silky veils and other exotic imagery.

Greek Easter bread

Mahlab and mastic are two ingredients in this recipe that may be unfamiliar to many cooks. Mahlab or mahlep (the ground kernel of the black cherry) is used to flavour breads and pastries, while mastic is the resin of the acacia tree and must be pulverised before using as a flavouring. Both mahlab and mastic are available at Greek delicatessens.

300 ml milk

½ cup sugar

30 g fresh yeast

4 eggs

8 egg yolks

1 teaspoon salt

few drops vanilla

½ teaspoon ground cardamom

2 teaspoons mahlab (optional)

½ teaspoon mastic (optional)

1 kg plain flour

300 g butter, softened

1 dozen red eggs

EGGWASH

1 whole egg

pinch of salt

🕊 MAKES 3 LOAVES

Warm the milk and add the sugar and yeast. Beat the eggs and egg yolks and add to the milk with the salt and vanilla. Add the cardamom, and the mahlab and mastic, if using.

Add the liquid to the flour and work to a dough in a machine fitted with a dough hook, or knead by hand for 10 minutes until smooth and elastic. Spread the dough into a rectangle and spread on the butter. Roll up and either knead until fully incorporated or return to the machine and beat, using a flat K beater, until smooth. Place the dough in a lightly greased bowl, cover with plastic film and allow to double in size.

When risen, divide the dough into nine pieces. Roll each piece into a long rope and plait three pieces at a time to make three long plaits. Shape the plaits into circles. Tuck four red eggs into each loaf and allow to rise again. Preheat the oven to 175°C and lightly grease a baking sheet (or sheets).

Make the eggwash by beating the egg and salt together. Place the loaves on the baking sheet, brush the loaves with the eggwash and bake for 30 minutes.

OPPOSITE AND RIGHT   The red dye used to colour the eggs is available at any European delicatessen during the Easter period. Use a stainless steel saucepan, as the dye leaves a hard-to-remove stain in aluminium pots. Children love to dip the eggs and can also help push the dyed eggs into the uncooked bread dough for the Easter loaf.

LUNCH PREPARATIONS

I have shared many breakfasts with Janni and his partner, David, on their sun-dappled balcony. This time we set up the breakfast table as a work station and Elena joined in to share the work and listen to the stories. It should be said that Sydney did not live up to its sunny reputation – the wind blew hard and cold and the sun proved very elusive. As Janni reminded us, an Easter picnic in Greece would probably be at least as blustery!

Janni had some grapevine leaves he had pickled in the early summer so we were soon wrapping dolmades and tucking them firmly in a pan. We reminisced that this had been a very popular appetiser at Stephanie's Restaurant years ago and Janni had always needed to protect the savoury rolls from marauding cooks. He had used tomato juice to cook them rather than the more traditional egg and lemon sauce. But, as he explained to Elena, he had not forgotten the egg and lemon sauce. It had reappeared on his menu recently in a different dish, as a frothy sabayon with lightly warmed oysters. To finish our morning preparation and lesson Janni tucked some red eggs into a spiced brioche loaf and baked it.

THE PICNIC

All the provisions were packed up in a basket, and laden with basket and rugs, glasses, bottles and other essentials, we set off for our picnic, carried across the water by Janni and David's friend Garnet Kinlay in his yacht, *Cyrene*. Garnet's four-year-old daughter Madeleine also came along. What a stylish way to arrive! Stella showed us how to clink our eggs together and say *Christos Anésti!* ('Christ is risen!') and to reply *Alithós O Kyrios!* ('It is true He has risen!'), and she recounted the Old Testament story of Martha and her basket of eggs. The semolina halva was a glorious finale. And then a watery sun broke through the clouds.

BELOW   We reached windy Shark Island after setting off from the wharf in the *Cyrene*. The picnic table was soon groaning with beautiful food.

OPPOSITE, CLOCKWISE FROM BELOW LEFT Olive-branch decorations and wine glasses on the table; Anthony Puharich, Elena, Janni and Stephanie; Stella Cheirdari; wild weed pie; a heavy picnic basket; the table laden with food.

PICNIC MENU

❧

Sea urchins
Dolmades and olives

❧

Wild weed pie with
homemade filo pastry

❧

Leg of lamb slow-baked
in a paper parcel,
with preserved lemon
and garlic
Greek salad

❧

Stella's semolina halva
Easter bread with red eggs

❧

Wines
Laxaridis Chateau
Julia 1997
Boutari Merlot
Xinamavro 1995
Samos Dessert Wine

tropical

spirit

Noosa and Its Hinterland

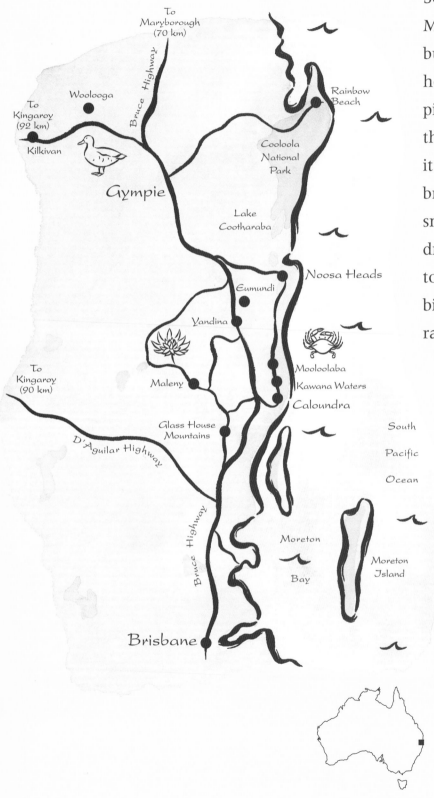

Some call Noosa Heads a suburb of Melbourne. I don't know about that but it is a very special subtropical holiday destination and a much-loved piece of paradise for those who live there all year round. It seems to have it all. On Main Beach, gentle rollers break onto an endless stretch of smooth white sand. Nature is more dramatic on Sunshine Beach, a little to the south, where the waves are bigger and can be expected to crash rather than uncurl.

People are out early at Noosa, walking, jogging or just enjoying a coffee at one of several cafes situated right alongside the sand. All manner of craft, large and small, dot the length of the Noosa River before it flows into the sea at Laguna Bay. There is splendid saltwater and freshwater fishing in the inlets, estuary and river. Magnificent Noosa National Park is reached from the town via a boardwalk, the start of which edges the Main Beach foreshore, and there are over 470 hectares of bushland to explore along well-marked trails. And of course there is Hastings Street, bursting with fashion and recreational opportunities, not to mention restaurants, cafes and ice-cream parlours. All this plus a lush hinterland, its inhabitants occupied with growing much of the food enjoyed in Noosa (and elsewhere) and their small townships resolutely rural as opposed to the seductive froth and bubble of Hastings Street.

And everywhere is a landscape that mixes and contrasts the familiar with tropical overtones: slender drooping-leafed gum trees on one side of the road, thick stands of sugar cane on the other, huge mango trees and laughing kookaburras, pandanus palms and quarrelling pink and grey galahs. I was startled to see a luxuriant purple bougainvillea climbing high into the branches of a gum tree and somehow the image of a farmer wearing a purple satin waistcoat over his work clothes came to mind.

PREVIOUS PAGES   The spectacularly beautiful lotus paddy at Hans Erken's permaculture farm near Maleny.
BELOW   Hot pink and blazing orange are very much the colours of Noosa, seen here in bright bougainvillea (left) and orchids.

The temperature rarely falls below 22°C during the day and the evenings are mild. But the weather can be very dramatic. On one visit a farmer told me they had had 7 inches (178 millimetres) of rain in the last two weeks, and one of those inches had fallen minutes before I arrived. On this visit we dodged the rain every day and were told that there had been 60 inches (152.4 centimetres) of rain since January, four months ago. I enjoyed the evening spectacle of a dramatic sound-and-light performance of lightning, dancing over the dark sea while the thunder rolled before the rains came. And I was lulled to sleep by a full-throated choir of frogs. I woke to a Noosa newly washed, sparkling in warm sunshine with every leaf gleaming.

Tourism is the most important industry in the region and the local council insists that all development and planning must maintain Noosa's distinctive character, perceived as a mix of sophisticated lifestyle and natural beauty. The history of Noosa Heads as a holiday resort is fascinating. Originally the white settlers came to the region for logging and for the goldfields at Gympie, 50 kilometres away. Its reputation as a good fishing spot grew and many of those who stayed were fishermen. Guesthouses offered creature comforts to some of the fishermen, and early tourists took cruises up the river in riverboat ferries.

By the 1960s and 1970s Noosa Heads had been discovered by the young and adventurous. The hippie trail that stretched from Kathmandu through Indonesia had a little outpost at Noosa and in the hills just beyond. Many of these cheerful young people stayed on to make an indelible impression on the character and importance now given to the great food in the area. They brought energy, a lust for life, and an appreciation of fresh seafood. Some are still there, some have sons and daughters working in the business of feeding people, and they are still having fun!

SAND CRABS

Commercial fishing is Queensland's fifth-largest primary industry, and the crab industry has a combined value of $18.4 million annually. Crabbing has always been a traditional holiday activity and members of the public are permitted to sink four pots per person per day. Professional crab fishermen work on a somewhat larger scale.

Glen and Brett | *I spoke with Glen Adamson who, with his son Brett, has a successful business catching both spanner* (Ranina ranina) *and sand crabs* (Portunus pelagicus). The Adamsons fish out of Kawana Waters, adjacent to Mooloolaba, just 45 kilometres south of Noosa Heads. In Victoria and South Australia sand crabs are known as blue swimmer crabs, and in Western Australia as manna crabs (and, said the irrepressible Glen, they are known by several other names when they get you with their strong nippers). Both Glen and Brett are qualified women's hairdressers as well as professional fishermen – an unusual combination of skills!

Brett is the skipper of his 10-metre boat *Rodi*, and Glen acts as his 'deckie' and is also responsible for the back-up onshore work. There is a canal system that snakes behind ordinary-looking suburban streets, which comes as a complete surprise to strangers – the *Rodi* is tied up at the end of the drive much as one might park the family car. The canals are rich in fish and Glen assured me that one could toss a line from the mooring pontoon any time and catch a bream or sand whiting.

Glen and Brett usually fish about one hour's travelling time offshore. The crab pots are left overnight and collected the next day. The men expect to catch around 80 kilograms of sand crab a day, almost all of which are cooked on board in sea water and then distributed to local restaurants and other outlets via a distributor. The spanner crabs are mostly exported live to Taiwan. Modern technology has taken almost all of the chance from commercial fishing, leaving the way open for an unscrupulous operator to be greedy. The industry is therefore closely regulated to prevent overfishing and pot limits apply. Professional crabbers are allowed fifty pots per day. A good sand crab will feel heavy in the hand and weigh around 650 grams.

Elena and I joined Glen and Brett early one morning and tested our sea legs. The ocean was quite rough and the boat pitched and rolled but our anxieties faded as the pots were winched to the surface and the snapping crabs were released into baskets to be sorted and measured. All females are thrown back and no crab can be taken that measures less than 15 centimetres across the top shell. The catch is put straight into a tub of ice slurry so the crabs go to sleep before they are tipped into a pot of boiling water. They die instantly with no distress and no shedding of legs.

OPPOSITE AND BELOW   Glen Adamson empties sand crabs out of the pot and shows us two of the snapping beauties. The catch goes into an ice slurry before being cooked on board the boat. The ice is an important factor in maintaining the quality of the crabs prior to cooking.

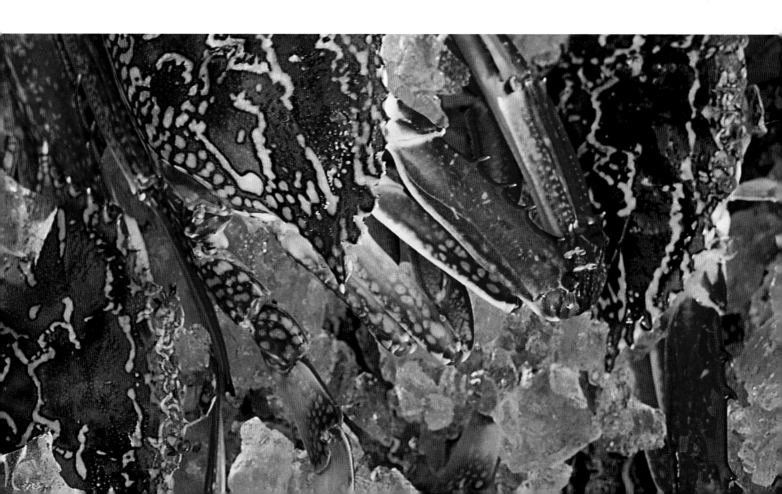

Glen has little demand for green (uncooked) crab and says that the tradition is still strong in Queensland to serve freshly cooked crab and bread and butter and just go for it! Glen showed us the fastest way to pick crabmeat from the shell, a true labour of love. We weighed the crab before and after and a 550-gram crab yielded 200 grams of meat. After our lesson we lunched on another simple Queensland treat – crab sandwiches. Fresh wholemeal bread, well buttered, bulging with just-caught and freshly picked crab. They were sensational.

I enjoy tackling a whole crab when sitting around in shorts and a T-shirt, but there are times when it is wonderful to have had the work done for you. An offer of sunshine, fresh crab, lime juice and a crisp white wine will get me anytime! Other combinations that work well with freshly boiled crabmeat are avocado, chilli, fresh herbs – especially coriander, basil or Vietnamese mint – and something crunchy, such as salad leaves, shredded green papaya (pawpaw), freshly dug water chestnuts or fresh bamboo shoots. All of these ingredients are grown on the Sunshine Coast, not all at the same time of the year though.

Fried stuffed blue swimmer crab

I cannot resist sharing this idea for enjoying blue swimmer crab. It involves Asian flavourings that are perfect in subtropical Noosa, but do not restrict the dish to holiday time. One can buy small packets of coconut cream but if they prove difficult to find, open a can of coconut milk and without shaking it up first, spoon the thick cream off the top. Transfer the rest of the milk to a screw-top jar and store in the refrigerator.

4 blue swimmer crab shells, cleaned
2 egg whites, stiffly beaten
vegetable oil
fresh lime wedges
sweet chilli sauce for dipping

STUFFING
30 g cellophane noodles
2 cups picked crabmeat (from 4 crabs)
1 fresh chilli, seeded and finely chopped
(or more to taste)
2 spring onions, very finely chopped
2 tablespoons coconut cream
2 teaspoons fish sauce
1 tablespoon finely chopped fresh coriander
leaves and stems

SERVES 4

To make the stuffing. Pour boiling water over the noodles and allow to stand for 3–4 minutes. Drain well and cut the noodles with scissors into 2 cm pieces. Mix the noodles in a bowl with all the remaining stuffing ingredients.

Pack the stuffing into the crab shells. Spoon the egg white over each shell and deep-fry the filled crab shells in plenty of hot oil until the egg white is golden brown. Serve hot and offer lime wedges and a small saucer of sweet chilli sauce.

AVOCADOS AND LIMES

Sandra and Ian | *Sandra and Ian Harding of Gold Creek Farm left high-pressured jobs in Melbourne nine years ago to embrace the lifestyle advantages in Eumundi, a most attractive tourist town some fifteen minutes' drive from Noosa Heads.* The Hardings' farm produces Tahitian limes and several varieties of avocado, with new ventures into hydroponic capsicums and basil.

Avocados were originally planted in the area in the 1930s to act as windbreaks before the potential of the fruit was fully grasped. In Ian's opinion there is still a great deal that needs to be done to increase the awareness and appreciation of this marvellous fruit. Each avocado contains as much fibre as a large grapefruit and is rich in vitamins C, B and folate. The Hardings' dog, Kandy, certainly enjoys them.

Gold Creek Farm avocados are all sold direct to restaurants, with the advantage that the chef can be certain that the fruit will be as he wants it – fully ripe today or ripe in two days, and for Ian and Sandra the vagaries of wholesale distribution and transportation are avoided. Ian guarantees the ripeness and delivers twice a week.

BELOW LEFT   The crabs look just as dramatic after cooking, when the blue markings turn scarlet.
BELOW RIGHT   Avocados mature on the tree but will only ripen off the tree. Mature avocados can remain hanging for several weeks, allowing the grower to pick only what is needed at a given time.

Avocados mature on the tree. Maturity is measured by the oil content in the fruit, which ensures a good flavour. However, the ripening process only commences once the fruit is picked and stored in temperature-controlled conditions. By picking his avocados fully matured, the oil content is high so the avocados taste rich and buttery. Ian says that an avocado that tastes watery has almost certainly been picked too early, a stringy avocado indicates a poor variety and one with little hard lumps in the flesh is the result of insect damage.

Gold Creek Farm is committed to non-toxic agricultural methods and Ian and Sandra firmly believe that this is the way of the future. Insects are not the worst threat they face – each year they wait nervously for the end of the winter when at any time a hailstorm can knock off all the new blossom from the limes and avocados, thus destroying the next crop and damaging fruit already hanging on the trees. The threat of hail was one of the reasons for deciding to grow some hydroponic crops. The capsicums and basil are protected from the elements and thrive.

On this warm day, steamy after the torrential rain of the night before, the air was heavy with the scent of lime blossom. The Hardings produce more limes than their restaurant customers can use so the fruit is also sold to selected retailers. I was intrigued to hear that the second crop of the year ripens in September, when there is a huge demand for limes from Melbourne for the Spring Racing Carnival! Some retailers sell limes by a unit price but request smaller fruit and pay the grower the same price per box whatever the fruit size. Ian is not fooled by this tactic and will not supply fruit below a certain size. The fruit is just as juicy and flavoursome when it grows to the size of a lemon. This is interesting for the consumer to realise and I for one have often purchased limes that are very small, probably too small I now realise. And a lime that has turned yellow is an old lime.

OPPOSITE   The crab salad looked lovely on our luncheon table, which echoed the colours of Noosa.

Crab salad

sea salt

1 hot chilli, seeded and finely chopped

1 tablespoon Vietnamese mint, chopped

1 tablespoon basil, chopped

lime juice

600 g picked crabmeat (about 4 good-sized crabs)

2 avocados, peeled and cut into chunks

🦀 SERVES 6

Mix the sea salt, chilli, herbs and lime juice and lightly toss the crab with this dressing. Add the avocado chunks and spoon the salad onto plates (or banana leaves cut into plate-sized pieces).

I adore fresh crab and wherever I am offered a fresh crab salad I order it. Over the years I have made many versions – but on a boat, on holiday, with fresh avocados and fresh limes at hand, it seems that simple is probably best, as in this recipe.

EXOTIC LEAVES, FLOWERS AND ROOTS

Hans | *Hans Erken of Earthcare Enterprises is another specialist grower who supplies direct to restaurants, in his case very well-known and up-market establishments in Sydney that can afford the not inconsiderable prices for his crops.* His permaculture farm at Crystal Waters is not far from Maleny, in the Sunshine Coast hinterland. Permaculture is an approach which aims to establish sustainable and energy-efficient systems that are both aesthetically pleasing and multifunctional. Hans offered to explain more if I had a month to spare!

The prevailing weather pattern seemed to be beautiful mornings and wet afternoons, so we started out from Noosa in the dark and had the pleasure of seeing a pink and pearly dawn light up the puffy clouds. Our drive took us past the spectacular Glass House Mountains, through lush green valleys and up steep hills offering the most beautiful vistas.

On my first visit several months previously I had sloshed through Hans' paddy fields (feeling very liberated in my gumboots) to look at where the water chestnuts would soon be shooting. On this subsequent visit the reedy tops of the

water chestnuts were dying down. Hans told me that the water chestnuts need to remain in the mud for a month after the tops have died to sweeten before harvesting, and that the harvested bulbs/tubers can last for over a year if stored in damp, cool sand providing there is no damage to the skin. This relatively small field was expected to yield 700 kilograms. On the earlier occasion, alongside the water chestnuts the lotus flower stems had just started to rise up above the water and the green round leaves had not yet grown to their spectacular full size. A graceful heron flew low over the flooded paddy.

On this later visit the lotus paddy was spectacular. There were full-blown flowers, tightly furled buds, and some in between. The juvenile leaves were heart-stoppingly beautiful, a rusty plum colour fading to emerald green. A drop of rain-water was trapped in the centre of some leaves where it glistened and rolled like a solitaire diamond. This particular lotus was a native variety, gathered from the nearby Mary River. Last year in Vietnam I had tasted a delicious salad made from the shredded flower stems of lotus but the stems of the Vietnamese lotus were much more fleshy than this variety.

ABOVE   Hans dug us a clump of Thai ginger known as Chinese Keys, or *kra chaai* *(Boesenbergia panduratum)*. In this case it is not the bumpy rhizome that is eaten but the finger-like roots that form from it. The flavour is aromatic and faintly camphor-like, without the hotness of regular ginger.

OPPOSITE   Hans's Moso beautiful bamboo grove is a tranquil place.

We moved on to the bamboo grove and to the gingers. Like palm hearts, fresh bamboo shoots bear little resemblance to the canned product. Where both are flabby and dull of colour in the can, when fresh they are crisp and juicy, the heart of palm being white and the bamboo shoot a pale cream. I had never seen a bamboo shoot being harvested and was therefore most intrigued to see how the tiny tip pushed through the soil, just like a mushroom. Each clump of bamboo is made up of various stalks, correctly known as culms, and produces many shoots. The shoots are dug out of the ground early in the morning and flown directly to Sydney, to be enjoyed within the next two to three days. Further trimming is necessary, which means that only about 50 per cent of the shoot is finally edible. An expensive delicacy.

We stroked the soft velvet of the juvenile Moso bamboo. As the trees get older this softness becomes more like a fine sandpaper to touch. Hans was told by a Japanese friend that for spiritual and physical wellbeing one should take a bottle of sake to a Moso bamboo grove before dawn, dig a shoot, wrap slices of it in toasted seaweed and enjoy the sounds of the wind sighing in the leaves, the warmth of the sake and the textures and flavours of the just-picked bamboo shoot.

We gathered Vietnamese mint, betel leaf, chillies and basil, and kaffir lime leaves, admiring the knobbly fruit of this tree – which, although virtually without juice, has a thick zest that is lovely added to dishes – and last but not least some of the smooth ivory lotus tubers. These last were to make into deep-fried chips to garnish our duck.

I found this visit most exciting. Not only did I get to touch, smell and taste new things, but I could immediately see how such flavours would complement the dishes we were planning. It was an enjoyable lesson in cooking in harmony with a particular environment.

It is interesting that there is only a very small demand from the many restaurants in Noosa Heads for these exotic flavours being grown right on their doorstep. There are other growers of exotic leafy herbs and chillies but Hans has the most exotic and scientifically managed collection of any I saw or heard about. His Internet web site is very impressive, he travels extensively and he is invited around the world to talk about the whys and wherefores of permaculture.

Ground fish with betel leaves

Pla Bon, as this dish is known, is a very ancient Thai snack that was first recorded in the court of King Narai in the late seventeenth century. David Thompson of Sydney's Darley Street Thai and Sailor's Thai restaurants finds that it is best made from flathead enriched with a little smoked trout, but any fish will do. The ingredients are tossed, combined and thrown onto a few betel leaves. Traditionally, the fish meal would be served in a bowl surrounded by various accompaniments. If betel leaves are not available, you can use young spinach, butter lettuce or coral lettuce as an alternative.

1 x 200 g flathead fillet

salt

1 small piece smoked trout

1 cup oil

3 slices galangal

3 tablespoons white granulated sugar

½ cup crispy fried shallots (sold in packets at Asian grocers)

4 red shallots, sliced

3 tablespoons fish roe (optional but sumptuous)

FOR SERVING

mandarins

pomelo

watermelon

half-ripe mangoes

betel leaves

fresh coriander sprigs

SERVES 6

Preheat the oven to 180°C. Soak the fish fillet in water with a large pinch of salt for 10 minutes. Drain and place on a cake rack on a foil-lined tray. Roast until firm and beginning to colour – in fact, until it is almost over-cooked – and remove from the oven.

Grind the fish with 1 tablespoon salt and the smoked trout in a food processor until the fish looks like fresh breadcrumbs. Heat the oil in a wok and add the galangal. Pour in the fish crumbs and stir constantly to prevent them from clumping. Fry over medium heat until the mixture has lost its raw fishy smell and becomes toasty and golden. Drain in a strainer and then spread out to drain further on absorbent paper. Leave to cool. The crumbs will last 3–4 days unrefrigerated, but are at their best on the day.

In a small bowl, combine the crumbs with 1 teaspoon salt, the sugar and the fried shallots. The mixture should taste surprisingly sweet, and salty. Finish with the red shallot and the fish roe. Serve in a bowl surrounded by the cleaned, segmented and sliced fruits, betel leaves and coriander sprigs.

Chicken coconut and kra chaai

Turmeric leaves can be bought in Asian markets. If they are not available on the day, the rice can be flavoured with a couple of kaffir lime leaves, or with a few slices of ginger, or in any other way that takes your fancy.

1 chicken, jointed but pieces still on the bone
12 pieces *kra chaai*, scrubbed but not peeled
6 kaffir lime leaves
zest of 2 kaffir lime fruit
juice of 2 Tahitian limes
400 ml coconut milk
salt
1–2 fresh chillies, seeded and sliced *or*
    freshly ground black pepper
fish sauce
2 tablespoons coconut cream (from top of
    unshaken can of coconut milk)
fragrant rice cooked with young turmeric leaves
2 handfuls fresh coriander leaves

SERVES 3–4

Place the first eight ingredients in a heavy-based pot and bring to simmering point. Reduce the heat and simmer very gently until the chicken is tender (approximately 45 minutes). Taste the sauce and adjust the flavour with fish sauce. Add the coconut cream and stir into the pot. Reheat but do not boil or the sauce will curdle.

Cook the rice in the usual way. Lay the fresh turmeric leaves on top of the rice at the beginning of the process, either in a covered pot or in a rice cooker. Discard the leaves at the end of the cooking time. Serve the chicken with the coriander leaves and the fragrant rice.

OPPOSITE   Betel leaves (*Bai champluu*) are closely related to the betel nut. The leaf has a slightly acidic orange flavour.
BELOW   The fruit of the kaffir or makrut lime (*Citrus hystrix*) has little juice but its zest is wonderfully fragrant.

Lotus stem and prawn salad

In Ho Chi Minh City in 1998 I watched an outstanding demonstration by chef Madame Nguyen Dzoan Cam Van, who showed us how to create a salad using pork, prawns and fresh lotus stems. Tony Tan, our tour leader, assured us that we could obtain fresh lotus at Asian markets in Australian cities, but he added that one could consider using finely sliced raw artichokes or even celery to add crunch.

In Vietnam we were served very freshly fried prawn crackers with this dish, as well as a fish sauce for dipping made by simmering together 1/2 cup fish sauce with 3/4 cup white sugar until it had the texture of honey.

This recipe calls for Vietnamese pickles, most of which are not labelled in English so you need to take potluck. They vary enormously, but it is the piquant and sharp taste that is needed in this salad.

500 g lotus stems
juice of 1 lemon
75 g sugar
100 g carrot, cut into julienne
200 g cooked lean pork, thinly sliced
200 g cooked pig's ear, thinly sliced
100 g cooked prawns, peeled
basil *or* sawtooth coriander, chopped
1 onion, finely sliced and soaked in a little rice vinegar
1 hot red chilli, seeded and finely sliced (or more to taste)
50 g Vietnamese pickles (experiment!)
fish sauce
a little extra lemon juice

50 g crispy fried shallots (sold in packets at Asian grocers)
100 g roasted unsalted peanuts, roughly chopped

🍳 SERVES 8

Cut the lotus stems in half lengthwise and then cut the halves into pieces 5 cm long. Soak in the lemon juice for 15 minutes, drain well and toss with two-thirds of the sugar. Leave for 30 minutes and then drain. Toss the carrot in the remaining sugar, leave for 15 minutes and drain.

In a large bowl toss the pork, prawns, drained carrot and lotus stem, herbs, drained onion, chilli and Vietnamese pickles. Mix well and season with the fish sauce and extra lemon juice to taste. Pile onto a serving dish and scatter the fried shallots and roasted peanuts over the top. If desired, some of the pork and prawns can be reserved for the final garnishing.

Tony's lotus root sandwiches

OPPOSITE   The smooth, ivory tubers of lotus root with a selection of aromatics from Hans Erken's garden. Clockwise from below left are hot chillies, curry leaves, Vietnamese mint and betel leaves. To make lotus root crisps, slice fresh lotus root very thinly and deep-fry until crisp. Drain well and serve as an appealing garnish with any vaguely Asian meat, poultry or fish dish.

White miso is sold in packets and is not to be confused with regular miso paste.

100 g white miso paste
1 teaspoon finely chopped ginger
1 clove garlic, finely chopped
4 x 1 cm thick slices lotus root
4 sheets toasted nori seaweed
vegetable oil

🍳 MAKES 4

Mix the white miso paste with the ginger and garlic. Stuff the cavities of the lotus slices with the paste. From the nori sheets, cut squares that are a little larger than the diameter of the lotus root. Sandwich the stuffed lotus root between two squares of nori. Heat the oil in a pan or wok to a moderate heat and fry for 2 minutes on each side until the nori is crisp. Serve at once.

THE HINTERLAND DUCK

John and Christa | *John and Christa Douglass operate Bendele Farm at Kilkivan, nearly two hours north-west of Noosa.* John Douglass says he has been involved in growing ducks for forty-five years. He also says he was a bouncer in a hotel for a while. He has a twinkle in his eye and a great sense of humour. It must be the ducks. He loves them. At the end of the day he says he often takes a beer and goes and sits in the shade and watches his ducks. 'I learn a lot from them about life, about behaviour,' he told me.

He and his wife bought their present property two years ago and John finds it just about perfect for ducks. He draws plenty of clear fresh water from his bores, the lifeblood of all farming. His biggest problems are caused by predators: foxes, dingoes and crows. Dingoes take the young lambs – they had taken seventeen the previous week – and the crows dive on the tiny yellow ducklings. They lose interest in the birds once they grow their first feathers. John likes his birds to range wherever they like and their feed contains no growth hormones or antibiotics and no harmful pesticides are used on the farm. Christa is very interested in the use of herbs and some of the duck yards are edged with comfrey, mugwort and millet, all of which the ducks seem to enjoy. John ensures that the birds also eat some garlic and lucerne. He ponders the question of whether the birds distinguish flavours or whether they will eat anything indiscriminately. Like so many farmers I meet, he believes that increasingly the market will demand, and certainly prefer to buy, food that is perceived as 'clean', so that even if one were motivated by market forces rather than principle the incentive is still there.

The ducks John is breeding are a cross between a Pekin, an Aylesbury and a Rouen, and have a deep breast and very tender legs. He is aiming for a bird that has plenty of breast development and not too much fat. He will not let the ducks swim in the dam because it toughens their chest and legs, but they do stroll in the early-morning grass when it is wet with dew or rain. 'A short life but the best possible one' seems to be John's motto.

His concern continues through to processing. John and Christa process all the birds they grow on their farm. He has designed a soft plucker to minimise damage to the skin of the bird. Almost every bit of the duck is sold – including the liver, the fat and the bones. The down and feathers are exceedingly valuable and are sold to make quilts to snuggle into. 'I'd shear them if I could,' John joked.

Max's barbecued duck salad

At our lunch Elena and I were assisted in our outdoor 'kitchen' by Max Porter, a friend and fellow chef. Max has a restaurant at Noosaville called Native Sun, subtitled 'Food of no fixed address', and he does have a very free-wheeling mind when finding inspiration for his dishes. His speciality is duck, which he calls Duck My Way. (It was Max who had first introduced me to John Douglass so it was fitting that Max was on hand to help toss the lunch ducks in the wok.) Kecap manis, an Indonesian soy sauce used in this recipe, is widely available.

SAUCE

1 cup hoisin sauce

1 cup kecap manis

4 tablespoons medium-sweet sherry

4 tablespoons honey

50 g sugar

2 cloves garlic, finely chopped

water

SALAD

½ Chinese cabbage, finely shredded

2 medium-sized carrots, peeled and grated

250 g fresh bean sprouts

12 coriander leaves, torn

12 mint leaves, torn

handful pea tendrils *or* shoots

1 medium-sized salad onion, finely cut
  on the diagonal

½ bunch green spring onions *or* scallions,
  finely chopped

250 g dry chow mein noodles

oil for frying

½ cup roasted peanuts

½ cup roasted cashews

2 ripe Roma tomatoes, sliced

½ continental cucumber, peeled and cut into
  short batons

1 whole roast duck, meat removed and thinly sliced

GARNISH

crispy fried shallots (sold in packets at Asian grocers)

green spring onions, finely sliced

red capsicum, thinly sliced

🌾 SERVES 4

To make the sauce. Combine all the ingredients, adding enough water to thin to a pouring consistency.

To make the salad. Mix the cabbage, carrot, bean sprouts, coriander, mint, pea tendrils, onion and spring onion together and cover with water. Place in the refrigerator for a couple of hours to crisp.

Reconstitute the noodles in warm water for 20 minutes. Drain and then fry the noodles in small batches. Allow them to cool, and then lightly crush them with your hands and set aside. Remove the crisped salad ingredients from the refrigerator and spin-dry. Add the peanuts, cashews, noodles, sliced tomato and cucumber.

Toss the duck slices until hot in a hot wok, adding a trace of oil (or rewarm in a microwave), and add to the salad. Add enough sauce to thoroughly moisten all the ingredients. Place in individual serving bowls and top with the fried shallots, sliced spring onion and capsicum strips. Drizzle over a little more of the sauce. Serve with a bowl of fresh chillies for those who wish to make their salad hot and spicy.

Crispy pressed duck

1 size 18–20 duck

light soy sauce

vegetable oil for deep-frying

MARINADE

200 ml Chinese red rice-wine vinegar

75 ml light soy sauce

1 tablespoon sugar

3 slices ginger, roughly chopped

1 clove garlic, roughly chopped

3 spring onions, sliced lengthwise and cut into
   2 cm pieces

2 whole star anise

1 cinnamon stick, lightly bruised

STIR-FRY INGREDIENTS

6 slices ginger, cut into julienne

fresh chilli slices to taste

2 kaffir lime leaves, finely shredded

1 clove garlic, finely sliced

4 thick slices fresh pineapple, cut into bite-sized
   pieces

1 sweet red capsicum, cut into pieces

½ cup fresh bamboo shoots, sliced into julienne,
   or fresh water chestnuts *or* kra chaai

½ cup chicken *or* duck stock

GARNISH

fresh coriander sprigs

lime wedges

SERVES 3–4

To prepare the duck. Remove the head, neck and feet, leaving some neck skin attached to protect the breast. Using poultry scissors, cut the duck in half down the centre of the breast and along each side of the backbone. Mix the marinade ingredients and marinate the duck for 8–12 hours. Remove and drain briefly.

To steam the duck. Place the duck halves skin-side uppermost on the perforated tray of a steamer (or place a colander over a pot of boiling water and cover the colander with a saucepan lid). Steam for 35–45 minutes until a skewer will slip easily through the thickest part of the thigh. While warm, extract all the bones. They should slip out easily. Fold each duck half over so that the breast side meets the thigh and leg side. You should have two neat parcels completely covered with duck skin. Wrap in plastic wrap, place on a tray or plate and press with a heavy weight for 24 hours.

To finish the duck. Unwrap the duck parcels and paint with light soy sauce. Heat the vegetable oil to very hot in a wok and slip in the duck halves. They will take about 5–8 minutes to become crisp and golden brown. Spoon the hot oil over them as they fry. Remove and drain on a paper-lined plate and reserve in a warm spot. Wipe out the wok, add a little fresh oil and quickly do the stir-fry.

To stir-fry. Heat the oil to very hot and toss in the ginger, chilli, lime leaves and garlic. Toss for a few seconds until fragrant. Add the pineapple, capsicum and bamboo shoots and toss for 5 minutes, keeping everything moving. Add a splash of stock and lower the heat to moderate. Place the lid on for 2 minutes while the duck is sliced into thick chunks and serve.

To serve. Each diner has a portion of vegetable, several duck chunks, a few sprigs of coriander and a lime wedge. For lunch we served a side dish of green papaya salad (see page 230).

This is a great dish in that all of the preparation is done one and a half days in advance and it just needs a flamboyant toss in the wok to finish off. The stir-fry ingredients are suggestions only. A simpler stir-fry would include seasonally available greens such as Chinese broccoli, snowpeas and so on.

Tropical bamboo species allowed to develop exposed to light are more likely to produce bitter shoots. If the shoot is bitter, it must be peeled, sliced finely and blanched in boiling water, then rinsed and simmered in more fresh water for 10 minutes. If the shoots are covered when first emerging and allowed to develop in darkness to a suitable size for harvesting, as for the Moso variety, there is virtually no bitterness. Canned bamboo shoots are not recommended.

OPPOSITE   Once the crispy duck dish was assembled it offered a satisfying balance of meatiness, crunch, juiciness, heat, sourness (lime juice) and sweetness (pineapple).

Green papaya salad

There are many ethnic variations of this salad. My recipe is intended to be eaten at once or the next day. It's great with barbecued prawns, too!

2 cloves garlic, finely chopped

1–2 hot chillies, seeded and chopped

3 cm piece ginger, chopped

1 teaspoon sugar (palm sugar gives the best flavour)

juice of 3 limes

1 ripe tomato, seeded and roughly chopped

2 teaspoons fish sauce

2 cups grated green papaya

3 tablespoons coriander leaves and fine stems

2 tablespoons raw peanuts, roughly chopped

🌿 SERVES 6

Traditionally one mashes the first six ingredients to a paste in a mortar, but a food processor can be used. Transfer the paste to a bowl and add the rest of the ingredients.

Thoroughly toss the salad, then taste for balance and adjust with fish sauce, lime juice and/or sugar.

Pickled pineapple relish

When there are no juicy golden pineapples to eat fresh, a jar of this relish is a great stand-by. It is also very good in a ham sandwich.

1 cup brown sugar

1½ cups white-wine vinegar

¼ cup preserved stem ginger, finely chopped

2 teaspoons yellow mustard seeds

1 teaspoon ground cinnamon

1 kg pineapple, weighed after peeling and trimming, cut into bite-sized chunks

½ cup currants

½ cup fresh lime juice

1 cup thinly sliced onion

2 tablespoons vegetable oil

2 hot chillies, seeded but left in whole pieces

1 tablespoon sea salt

🌿 MAKES APPROXIMATELY 1 LITRE

Combine the sugar, vinegar, ginger, mustard seeds and cinnamon in one bowl, and the pineapple, currants and lime juice in another. In a heavy-based stockpot sauté the onion in the vegetable oil with the chilli pieces until the onion is quite soft but not coloured. Add the pineapple, currants and lime juice and stir to coat. Add the sugar–vinegar mixture and the salt. Stir and cook on a low heat until all the sugar has dissolved. Bring to the boil, increase the heat and simmer briskly for about 15 minutes until the pineapple is translucent and soft. Cool and then discard the chilli. Bottle into clean dry jars and seal. Refrigerate after opening.

OPPOSITE   The green papaya salad is shown here in the smooth, polished curve of a spent palm leaf. The leaf fell from a young tree growing in the gardens of The Spirit House restaurant in Yandina.

TROPICAL FRUIT

Tropical fruit for breakfast is absolutely necessary when in Noosa. And for lunch – and why not for dinner too?

Sylvia and Scott | *At Highland Grove tropical fruit farm, a few minutes from Noosa, Sylvia and Scott Todd are growing more than fifty varieties of exotic fruits.* They planted their first exotic trees in 1979 as a hobby, having bought a farm that produced banana, papaya and custard apple. Now their biggest crop is lychees, of which 40 per cent is exported to Asia and the Pacific. The Todds are mildly surprised that the local restaurants are not more interested in the fruit they produce. And so am I. As a visitor I can think of no better dessert than a selection of perfectly ripe exotic fruit served with a wedge of fresh lime.

Sylvia served me a delicious small cake made from black sapote, a fruit also known very aptly as 'chocolate pudding fruit'. Scott described it less attractively as being like axle grease! One fruit has four times the amount of vitamin C as an orange. I have enjoyed black sapote in the far north simply halved and trickled with a little rum.

Custard apples are one of my favourites and they make stunning ice-cream. I had enjoyed outstanding fresh coconut ice-cream at Noosa Heads' premier ice-creamery, Massimo, and wondered whether Massimo would make us an ice-cream using custard apple for our lunch. Sylvia and Scott were happy to provide a spectacular selection of tropical fruit, for us to taste and for our guests to enjoy.

BELOW   The fruit we tasted at Highland Grove included the rollinia (left), which is related to the custard apple and has luscious, creamy flesh, and the small round abiu (right).

OPPOSITE   The mamey or black sapote is a most unusual fruit. On the tree it resembles some sort of prehistoric egg, as Elena suggested. The flesh inside is a deep orange and can be used to make excellent cup cakes, shown here decorated with chunks of ripe mango.

A new taste for me was abiu, a small round fruit that Sylvia described as tasting faintly of butterscotch. Elena said it reminded her of eating condensed milk. I found it quite exquisite, with a smooth creamy texture reminiscent of the rollinia, our next taste. Rollinias are related to custard apples but their flesh is slightly more acidic (Sylvia suggested lemon meringue) and the fragrance is delightful. Again a creamy, almost spritzig texture with a rich, deep flavour.

Black sapote cup cakes

150 g butter

1 cup sugar

3 large eggs

¼ teaspoon bicarbonate of soda dissolved in
   1 tablespoon boiling water

3 cups self-raising flour

pulp of 2–3 black sapote (about 1½ cups)

½ cup milk

mango slices for decorating

🕊 MAKES 24

Preheat the oven to 180°C. Cream the butter and sugar until fluffy and then add the eggs and the bicarbonate of soda. Add the flour and the fruit pulp alternately, folding through the mixture. Finally add the milk. Mix well.

Spoon into lightly buttered cup-cake containers, filling each one by two-thirds only. Add a piece of mango as decoration. Bake for 30 minutes. Test by inserting a fine skewer into the centre of one cake. If it comes out clean, remove the cakes to a wire rack to cool; if not, cook for a further few minutes until done.

Simple custard apple ice-cream

This recipe is reproduced with permission from *Thai Cuisine* by Mogens Bay Esbensen. The variety of custard apple known as a rollinia is ideal for dishes such as this as its flesh is particularly luscious.

3 medium-sized custard apples (or more as needed)
200 g castor sugar
2 eggs
2 tablespoons lime juice
2 cups cream

SERVES 8

Slice open the custard apples, scoop the flesh into a sieve and press it through, removing the seeds. Extract 3 cups of pulp and add the sugar. Beat the eggs with a fork and add to the pulp along with the lime juice. Whip the cream lightly and fold into the mixture. Churn until soft and creamy, and not too hard.

BELOW   Custard apple is just one of the flavours available at Massimo's ice-cream parlour in Noosa Heads. Elena and I certainly enjoyed our ice-creams!
OPPOSITE   At the lunch, we served Massimo's custard apple ice-cream topped with a sugared almond and accompanied by a selection of ripe fruit.

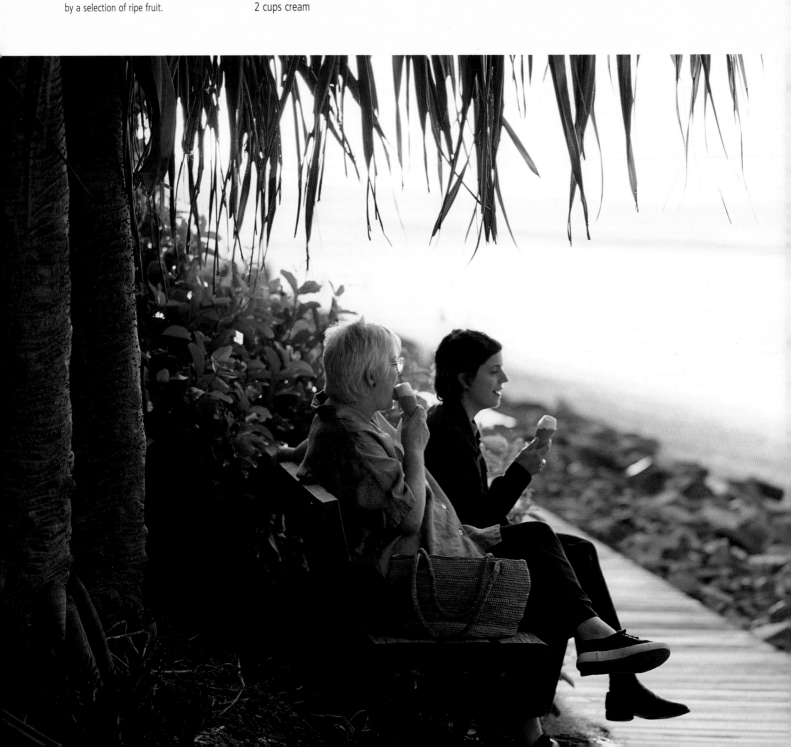

THE LUNCH

Our final lunch took place at The Spirit House restaurant at Yandina, another hinterland township about half an hour from Noosa Heads. It was the most perfect choice, with a series of long, low pavilions set in a tranquil garden overlooking a lotus pond, on which swam two pretty brown ducks. The Spirit House also has a busy cooking school, so the garden is not only a lovely place to wander but grows most of the herbs needed for the predominantly Asian-inspired dishes. Given that the classes are very popular, one might assume that the demand for Asian herbs and special crops will increase.

My assistant, Anna, and the production manager, Annie, did a spectacular job with the table. It was covered with metres of hot-pink cotton and down the centre were arranged banana leaves, giant hibiscus flowers in astonishing colours of burning hot pink, apricot and banana-yellow, with exotic fruits of all shapes, sizes and colours to fill in any gaps. One could not help but feel excited just looking at it. Elena, I noticed, had tucked a hibiscus flower behind her ear!

Places were set with terracotta plates lined with squares of banana leaf. All our suppliers were there, along with well-known Noosa identities Leonie Palmer of Ricky Ricardo's – one of the veterans of the restaurant scene at Noosa Heads – and her husband, Steven Fisher.

First we served the crab salad, so simple but so good. The ducks had been prepared and were now to be fried in hot oil. Separately we stir-fried some juicy pineapple and sweet red capsicum using exciting flavourings from Hans Erken's orchard – *kra chaai* ginger, kaffir lime leaf and chillies – and garnished the dish with little wafers of deep-fried lotus root.

After such a spicy dish, the creamy coolness of the custard apple ice-cream from Massimo was just right and there was much excitement at the tasting of so many exotic fruits. Many of the producers were meeting for the first time, so conversation tended towards farmer-speak of rain, freight costs, bureaucracy gone mad, licence fees, supply and demand and local demand. Promises were made to visit each other. I felt very pleased that we had facilitated some introductions that might lead who knows where.

OPPOSITE It is hard to think of a more delicious breakfast than ripe tropical fruit with a squeeze of lime.

OVERLEAF Our lunch table looked beautiful decorated with fruit and hibiscus blossoms in every shade of pink, gold, red and yellow.

MENU PAGE, CLOCKWISE FROM BELOW LEFT Leonie Palmer; looking onto the pond at The Spirit House; Max Porter (in dark blue shirt); Hans Erken and Stephanie; Max and Rhonette Porter; the wok at work.

LUNCHEON MENU

✍

Crab salad with avocado,
basil, Vietnamese mint,
chilli and lime juice

✍

Crispy pressed duck with
kra chaai ginger,
kaffir lime leaves,
pineapple and
sweet red capsicum

✍

Green papaya salad
with peanuts

✍

Custard apple ice-cream
with a selection of
tropical fruit

✍

Wines
Queensland Bald Mountain
Dry White 1997
Pibbin Adelaide Hills
Pinot Noir 1996

conversion table

LIQUID MEASUREMENTS

metric	imperial	
5 ml	$^1/_6$ fl oz	1 teaspoon
10 ml	$^1/_3$ fl oz	2 teaspoons
20 ml	$^1/_2$ fl oz	1 tablespoon
40 ml	1 fl oz	1 tablespoon + 2 teaspoons
60 ml	2 fl oz	$^1/_4$ cup
125 ml	4 fl oz	$^1/_2$ cup
250 ml	8 fl oz	1 cup

DRY MEASUREMENTS

metric	imperial
15 g	$^1/_2$ oz
28 g (25–30 g)	1 oz
40 g	$1^1/_2$ oz
50 g	2 oz
125 g	4 oz ($^1/_4$ lb)
150 g	5 oz
200 g	7 oz
225 g	8 oz ($^1/_2$ lb)
450 g	1 lb
500 g	1 lb 1 oz
1 kg	2 lb 2 oz

OVEN TEMPERATURES

Celsius	Fahrenheit
100°C	210°F
125°C	240°F
150°C	300°F
180°C	350°F
200°C	400°F
220°C	450°F
250°C	500°F

LINEAR MEASUREMENTS

metric	imperial
3 mm	$^1/_8$ in
5 mm	$^1/_4$ in
1 cm	$^1/_2$ in
2 cm	$^3/_4$ in
2.5 cm	1 in
5 cm	2 in

further reading

Alexander, Stephanie. *The Cook's Companion*. Viking, Ringwood, 1996.

— *Recipes My Mother Gave Me*. Viking, Ringwood, 1997.

— *Stephanie's Australia*. Allen & Unwin, Sydney, 1991.

— *Stephanie's Feasts and Stories*. Allen & Unwin, Sydney, 1988.

— *Stephanie's Journal*. Viking, Ringwood, 1999.

— *Stephanie's Menus for Food Lovers*. Mandarin Australia, Melbourne, 1991.

— *Stephanie's Seasons*. Allen & Unwin, Sydney, 1993.

Alexander, Stephanie and Beer, Maggie. *Stephanie Alexander & Maggie Beer's Tuscan Cookbook*. Viking, Ringwood, 1998.

David, Elizabeth. *English Bread and Yeast Cookery*. Penguin, Harmondsworth, 1979.

Esbensen, Mogens Bay. *Thai Cuisine*. Thomas Nelson, Melbourne, 1986.

Fisher, M.F.K. *Consider the Oyster*, in *The Art of Eating*. Vintage Books, New York, 1976.

Gloster, Michael. *The Shaping of Noosa*. Blue Group, Noosa Heads, 1997.

Gray, Patience. *Honey from a Weed*. Prospect Books, London, 1986.

Heuzenroeder, Angela. *Barossa Food*. Wakefield Press, Adelaide, 1999.

Hutchison, David (ed.). *A Town Like No Other: The Living Tradition of New Norcia*. Fremantle Arts Centre Press, South Fremantle, 1995.

Low, Tim. *Wild Food Plants of Australia*. Angus & Robertson, Sydney, 1991.

Nature & Culture: Proceedings of the Seventh Symposium of Australian Gastronomy, Canberra, ACT. Highland Press, Queanbeyan, 1993.

Palmer, Leonie. *Leonie Palmer's Noosa Cook Book*. Blue Group, Noosa Heads, 1996.

Roden, Claudia. *A New Book of Middle Eastern Food*. Penguin, Harmondsworth, 1986.

Solomon, Charmaine. *Encyclopedia of Asian Food*. William Heinemann Australia, Melbourne, 1996.

Studd, Will. *Chalk and Cheese*. Purple Egg, Melbourne, 1999.

Thiele, Colin. *Coorong*. Rigby, Adelaide, 1972.

Wallace-Crabbe, Chris. *Rungs of Time*. Oxford University Press, Melbourne, 1993.

Wolfert, Paula. *Good Food from Morocco*. John Murray, London, 1989.

index